Campobello:

Roosevelt's "Beloved Island"

Campobello:

Roosevelt's "Beloved Island"

STEPHEN O. MUSKIE

preface by Joseph P. Lash

Design: Guy Fleming

Composition: Camden Type 'n Graphics, Camden, Maine

Printing: Arcata Graphics, Kingsport, Tennessee

Published by
The Roosevelt Campobello International Park Commission
P.O. Box 97, Lubec, Maine 04652

THIS BOOK IS DEDICATED TO ALL THOSE READERS
WHO APPRECIATE BEAUTY IN ITS MANY FACETS,
WHETHER THEY BE OF NATURE OR OF MAN.
IF YOU SEARCH FOR BEAUTY ON CAMPOBELLO,
YOU WILL BE AMPLY REWARDED.

*Published in commemoration of the 100th anniversary
of the birth of FRANKLIN DELANO ROOSEVELT,
who was born January 30, 1882,
this book is an attempt to reveal some of what made Campobello
a special place for the president, who called it his "beloved island."*

Contents

Acknowledgments

No matter how independent I like to think myself, I could not have completed this book or the master's degree thesis which led to it without the help of many other people to whom I owe at least a debt of gratitude.

At the top of the list must be my wife, Lexi, whose patience and support never wavered over the past seven years since this project began. She accepted the great amount of time and money spent on the project with rarely a complaint. In fact, I think I complained more than she did.

My father was the first person to tell me about Campobello: a place where he feels completely relaxed and at home. If he hadn't been so enthusiastic about the island, I probably never would have gone there and discovered its magic for myself.

Of course the book would never have been published if it weren't for the support of the Roosevelt Campobello International Park Commission, especially James Rowe, an American member, and Roland Frazee, a Canadian member. To all of them I owe a special thank you. In their continuing, unselfish donation of their time and energy to maintain and improve the park they consistently demonstrate their affection for Campobello Island.

Three other people associated with the Roosevelt Park were also helpful. The late Rad Pike, former naturalist consultant to the park, and park superintendent Harry Stevens provided me with places to stay while I visited the area. I will always appreciate their advice and friendship. A former employee, Vera Calder, sometimes cooked for me, provided information about the island, and always had a smile, which was especially helpful whenever I felt frustrated about my work's progress.

Although I have thanked them before, in a less public way, I also want to recognize the support which many other people contributed to the completion of my original master of fine arts thesis project, upon which this book is based. Joe Albritton, Arnold Picker, and Edward Pizek provided invaluable support during and following my graduate school work. My three thesis advisors, Charlie Arnold, Mike Lewis, and Dave Robertson, contributed their time and suggestions which greatly improved the final thesis project. My former employer, Brian Thayer, and other friends at the *Biddeford-Saco Journal Tribune* provided support and many hours of assistance. Lou Jacques and Rita Murphy were especially helpful in setting the original thesis type. Kiki O'Connell and Mike Lafavore helped straighten out the narrative of the introduction.

Thanks go to all these people and many others I met at Campobello and Lubec, who helped in small but important ways.

FDR at the helm, off Campobello Island.
Courtesy of the Franklin D. Roosevelt Library

Preface

WHEN I read in Stephen O. Muskie's graphic account of Campobello Island, "Her air is tangy with the mixing scents of land and sea," it was almost as if one of the Roosevelts were speaking. "Lunch and a trip to Eastport," writes Eleanor in 1933, and continues, "with the engine breaking down as usual, and the rain in our faces for a time. . . . We came back in to tea before the fire. No telephone. Absolute peace. It is a joy."

"Campobello was next to Hyde Park in Father's affections," wrote his eldest son James in the engaging memoir *Affectionately, F.D.R.*, "It was his second home." And FDR himself, twelve years after his Campobello neighbors had discreetly engineered the transference of his polio-stricken body on a stretcher down the hill to a boat and then onto a train at Eastport, said on his return in 1933 aboard the *Amberjack II* at the end of the first "hundred days" of his presidency, "I was figuring this morning on the passage of time and I remembered that I was brought here because I was teething forty-nine years ago, I have been coming for many months almost every year until twelve years ago, when there. . . [was] a gap."

Franklin's mother and father, Sara and James, first visited Campobello in 1883, the year after Franklin was born, and immediately came under the enchantment of the "beloved island," as they called it. They bought several acres and ordered a house to be built for them. It was completed in 1886 and the Roosevelts soon were accepted as "permanent" summer residents. A few select families from the eastern seaboard summered on the island whose waters, despite their hazards, provided splendid anchorages for boats. James Roosevelt's first *Half Moon* sank on the way back to the Hudson and was followed by a second *Half Moon*, a 60-foot, two-masted schooner.

For the elderly James, the island's very tranquillity and seclusion gave it its attraction, but for the young Franklin it was the place where he learned to handle a boat in perilous waters, to fish and to swim, to lead "paper chases" along the cliffs and expeditions off the shores of Nova Scotia in search of pirates' buried loot. By the late 1890s he was organizing the summer residents' golf tournaments, the new sport. And in 1903 when he was courting Eleanor, he brought her and her maid to the island as his guests.

"I saw then," wrote Mrs. Hartman Kuhn, the Roosevelts' next-door neighbor at Campobello, "how he looked at you," and so she stipulated in her will that Sara could purchase the house for Eleanor and Franklin. It was a large one with thirty-four rooms, large and small, but after Eleanor's marriage it was the first house she felt was her own, and she loved furnishing it to her taste.

It had no electricity, was lit by kerosene lamps, and for decades there was no telephone, but that was part of its attraction for the two of them. Franklin entered politics in 1910 and Campobello became the one place where he could be with his family and the outside world was unable to get at him. As for Eleanor when she had Captain Franklin Calder take her up to St. Andrews in New Brunswick, in the "chig-chug," as the children called the motor launch, contentment echoed in every syllable as she wrote a friend, "The sun is out, and the fog is rolling out to sea, and I'm sitting in the bottom of the boat, sniffing salt air and now and then looking over the water to my green islands and gray rocky shores."

Between March 1905 when Eleanor and Franklin married and March 1916 when the youngest of six children, John, was born (one had died a few months after birth), Campo was the one place

FDR sailing with his father and Helen R. Roosevelt on The Half Moon,
1899. Courtesy of the Franklin D. Roosevelt Library

FDR with son Elliott at Campobello, 1911.
Courtesy of the Franklin D. Roosevelt Library

*FDR and Eleanor with the children and his mother, 1920. "Chief" is in front.
Courtesy of the Franklin D. Roosevelt Library*

*A family picnic on Campobello, 1912. FDR and Eleanor are in the center.
Courtesy of the Franklin D. Roosevelt Library*

Governor Francis Neptune of the Passamaquoddy Tribe meets with FDR at Campobello, 1920. Courtesy of the Franklin D. Roosevelt Library

FDR greets "my old friends at Campobello," June 29, 1933.
Courtesy of the Franklin D. Roosevelt Library

the children had "Pa" to themselves, and he and they loved it. There he taught all the children (but not Eleanor) to handle a boat, even in treacherous straits and narrows, took on the role of the nimble-footed hare and danced elusively ahead of them on strenuous "paper chases," picnicked and hiked and filled them with the lore of the place. It was no wonder that his son James described as "homesick-ness" his father's feelings for the island in the twelve years that his paralyzed limbs kept him from the annual trek to it.

The Roosevelts were like an army on the march when each year the household set out for Campobello. There was a nurse for each of the small children, three to five other domestics, mountains of trunks, valises, and hat boxes. They took a train to Boston, rested at old-fashioned Hotel Touraine during the day, took the sleeper to Ayers Junction in Maine, transferred to a wheezy train for the ride to Eastport, then went onto the motor launch for the last lap to Campo. "I know one Eleanor Roosevelt," wrote a friend, "who has four children [John would be born later that year] and moves them all six times a year — and does everything else besides."

Another feminist footnote: in 1935 when Eleanor took Emma Bugbee of the *New York Herald Tribune* with her to Campo-bello, she went on a sail with Captain Calder. Eleanor took the tiller from the Captain and explained to Emma, "I never get a chance to sail the boat myself. There are always many men around. . . . One has always to let the man do the sailing."

Franklin was the demon yachtsman. During the Woodrow Wilson administration when he was assistant secretary of the Navy, he sometimes turned up at Campobello aboard a destroyer. Al-though it was against naval regulations, he persuaded the captain to let him take the helm and piloted the ship at full speed ahead through fog-bound waters. The Bay of Fundy's tides and currents were bred into his bones. One of his pet dreams was to harness Pas-samaquoddy's precipitous tides for purposes of electric power. It was never realized, but perhaps the idea for the Rural Electrifica-tion Administration had its origin in those "eye-straining" nights by Campo's kerosene lamps.

The house was not much used in the thirties, but in 1941 and 1942 the president and Mrs. Roosevelt were delighted to have the International Student Service, on whose board Mrs. Roosevelt served, use it for its summer Student Leadership Institutes. A high moment at the Institute was the dance at Welshpool where Mrs. Roosevelt and an officer of the Royal Canadian Mounted Police led the company out onto the floor.

Ownership of the house was transferred to Elliott after the president's death. Eleanor spent most of the 1947 summer there in order to work on the second volume of her autobiography, *This I Remember*. Elliott later sold the house to the Hammer family who felt privileged to vacate it to allow Mrs. Roosevelt to use it. On such trips she stopped at Castine, Maine, to visit Bishop Will Scarlett, who had retired there, and his neighbor Molly Dewson, the fabled director of the Women's Division of the Democratic National Committee, not to mention a stop at Perry's Nuthouse in order to do some early Christmas shopping.

In the summer of 1962 she roused herself from her final illness to come to Campobello as President Kennedy's representative for the dedication of the FDR Memorial Bridge that linked the island with the mainland. Her friends David Gurewitsch and his wife flew up with her and the author's wife Trude drove down with her. She scarcely was able to get to her feet, and Trude wrote of her last day on Campobello, "For the first time that morning she walked up and down in front of the Campo house, 'so that I can manage the steps of the Scarlett house,' she said. . . . We drove down the Maine coast to do once more the things she always loved to do." A few weeks later she died.

"After speeches he came home and I think [he was] happy," she had written of Franklin's return to Campobello in 1933. She had the same happiness to be on the island. "[A] bit foggy," she wrote a friend. She was "settling down again into this quietest of places and loving it."

JOSEPH P. LASH

Left to right: *John, Franklin, Jr., FDR, and James sailing on the* Sewanna *on their cruise from Rockport, Maine to Campobello, July 14–28, 1936. Courtesy of the Franklin D. Roosevelt Library*

Campobello:

Roosevelt's "Beloved Island"

Separated by only a narrow tidal rip, Campobello Island is located only a stone's throw from Lubec, Maine, the easternmost town in the United States.

Introduction

S HE is shrouded by the cool, blue mist of early morning that slowly evaporates into the clean, bright air of midday. Her shore is shaped by the continual pounding of the icy surf from the Bay of Fundy, site of two great whirlpools and the highest tides in the world. Her air is tangy with the mixing scents of land and sea. The signs of man's presence are barely perceptible over much of her flowing fields, dense forests, tidal marshes, expansive mudflats, and jagged headlands. Campobello Island has changed comparatively little over the centuries that man has known her.

"The northern and southern ends of the island provide a dramatic topographical contrast. The north, with its ledge, thin topsoil and low hills, resembles the coast of Scotland. The south is almost tropical in the luxuriance of its ferns and flowers, culminating in the Fog Forest at Liberty Point, an eerie green-gray world of lichen-hung trees shrouded in perpetual fog."[1]

She seems so far away. Indeed she is far from the hurry-hurry rat race of society; removed from the mainstream; at the end of the cultural line, the technological line, the energy line, and the financial line.

To reach the end of that line, drive northeast along the Maine coast through countryside, becoming more sparsely populated as the miles roll by, toward the easternmost town in Maine: Lubec. Drive down the peninsula leading out to that town, along a ridge surrounded on three sides by an expanse of ocean and sky.

When you reach the road's end and look across the narrow slip of water separating her from the United States, there is Campobello.

She is a Canadian island, only a stone's throw from the United States; a mile by sea from her nearest Canadian neighbor, Deer Island; twelve miles by sea from the Canadian mainland. Her residents must drive over sixty miles of U.S. roads to reach the Canadian border and the city of St. Stephens, New Brunswick. For many years, because the only medical service available in the area was in Lubec, many Campobello babies were born in that Maine town, with the resultant right to choose their citizenship in the United States.

Geographically she should be a part of the United States. Yet the island is Canadian because of a purported historical quirk. As the story goes, Daniel Webster (1782–1852) led an American delegation for settlement of the boundary issue. Sailing down the St. Croix River, Webster, being a poor sailor, refused to continue farther into the rough seas of Passamaquoddy Bay to the east and around Campobello Island. Rather, he insisted on hugging the shore of Maine, through the Lubec Narrows, thus awarding the island to Canada.

Although it makes a colorful account of the manner in which Campobello came to be Canadian, Daniel Webster's stomach probably had little to do with the boundary decision. According to the proceedings of the Royal Society of Canada, "We cannot question that the line according to the usual customs in such cases would have followed the navigable channels, and would have given [the United States] Campobello, geographically a part of Maine and separated from it by only a narrow and shallow channel." That Canada was the island's recipient, "was due to no virtue on her part, but was a pure piece of luck. . . ."[2]

A long-dead tree frames the sky above Lake Glensevern, a barrier pond behind the beach at Herring Cove. President Roosevelt often swam here before contracting polio.

On a cool autumn morning, the light of the rising sun bathes Herring Cove beach in a warm yellow glow. Pilings of a fishing weir stretch from the beach into the cove.

Campobello was visited for thousands of years by Indians who left only huge piles of clam shells as evidence of their stays. Viking adventurers might also have touched her shores during one or more voyages. And the great French explorer Samuel de Champlain sailed through Passamaquoddy Bay on his way up the St. Croix River, the present boundary between the United States and Canada. On a map drawn by Champlain in 1607 he identifies Campobello as Port aux Coquilles (Harbor of Clams).

Five years after the first known settlement of the island by Europeans, "a census taken in 1689 listed its inhabitants as four men, four women, eight boys, five girls, four horses, and seven horned cattle."

But her recorded history really began about September 30, 1767, when the island was granted to Captain William Owen by Lord William Campbell, the British governor of Nova Scotia. Named the "Principal Proprietary of the Great Outer Island of Passamaquoddy," Owen chose to christen the island Campo Bello, as he said, "partly complementary and punning on the name of the governor," and partly in response to the island's beauty, "Campo Bello being, so I presume, the Spanish and Italian equivalent of the British fair field."[4]

Owen and his descendents ruled their little island kingdom, favorably or not, for the next 114 years. Under their rule, "the island was a feudal fief of a dynasty of Welsh seamen that gave the Royal Navy two admirals, one of whom was born on Campobello and the other of whom lies buried there."[5] Another was once the tutor of the English prime minister William Pitt.

"The Principal Proprietary was the island's lord, and the people were his tenants. His wife was given the courtesy title of Lady. He performed marriages. He prepared sermons and preached them in the church that he had caused to be built. He was inclined to regard the island's militiamen as his private army. The first Principal Proprietary erected a set of stocks and a whipping post to punish 'the unruly, disorderly and dishonest,' and his successors were all of them magistrates. At one point the Owens issued their own money emblazoned with the family motto Flecti Non Frangi (To be bent, not to be broken)."[6]

The fourth, and last, proprietary married into the family and changed his name to Owen, thus complying with a bequest which granted him title to the island. Seven years after his death the Owen era came to an end when his widow decided to sell her rights to Campobello to a group of American businessmen.

With $1 million in capital, they intended to develop the island into a summer resort to which wealthy, upper-class residents of New York, Boston, and Montreal could escape, traveling by private yacht or railway car. Although a boon to the island's economy, eventually "the resorts fell victim to a variety of factors, including the First World War, the motor car, the servant problem and the income tax."[7] But while it lasted, the resort community on the southern end of Campobello grew to include many spacious "cottages" and three prosperous hotels. Advertising brochures for the hotels described them as providing "all the comforts of a refined home," offering "quiet and retired life, made wholesome by the soft yet bracing air, never too hot and seldom too cold." They went on to say that at Campobello, "one may find absolute relief from hay fever."

Among the visitors to the island in 1883 were James and Sara Roosevelt, who brought with them their one-year-old son, Franklin, a future president of the United States. They liked the place so well that they bought ten acres of land overlooking Friar's

Bay and erected a cottage of their own.

Young Franklin Roosevelt spent his summers on the island, met his future wife, Eleanor, there, and in his fortieth year contracted polio there. That illness proved to be his greatest tragedy and the source of his greatest triumph in overcoming its debilitating physical and emotional effects.

"Campobello's contribution to the making of [Franklin Roosevelt] is considerable. His character, his courage and his humanity were developed there in formative years. When his place in world events and values is determined in the years to come these three qualities will be given high rank. Whatever the verdict of political history might be, the legends of Campobello will forever celebrate the adventures and habits of his boyhood. They helped Franklin Roosevelt gain the courage and self-reliance which scorned the handicaps of a great affliction."[8]

Because of his love of the island and its role in shaping his future, and thus the future of the United States, a tribute to his memory was developed on the island: the world's first international park.

The Roosevelt Campobello International Park was established in 1964 to preserve FDR's summer home and to give visitors the opportunity to experience some of what made Campobello a special place for him.

There are two proposed projects which could have enormous effects on the Roosevelt Park and on the ecology and economy of the island and the whole area. One is the construction of an oil refinery at Eastport, the only natural deep-water port on the east coast of the United States and, therefore, the only place suitable for the docking of crude-oil-carrying supertankers. The other project is a long-standing proposal for a tidal power facility to generate electricity.

Winter clouds, seemingly woven layer upon layer, drift slowly across the barren, snow-covered landscape of the Plains of Abraham, located in the Roosevelt Park's natural area on the southern end of Campobello Island.

Pilings of the former car ferry frame the town of Lubec, Maine, connected to Campobello since 1962 by the Franklin D. Roosevelt Memorial Bridge.

The refinery proposal has met considerable opposition on environmental grounds. For some time the United States Department of Environmental Protection has withheld necessary air and water quality permits for its construction. And the Canadian government has proposed regulations that would prevent travel of the supertankers through Head Harbour passage between Campobello and Deer Island. They say because of the narrow passage, the possibility of rough seas, and the persistent, heavy fog, there is great potential for a huge oil spill.

The tidal power project has been in existence for almost sixty years, having been actively encouraged by President Roosevelt following its conception by a Campobello neighbor of his, Dexter P. Cooper, an American engineer who came to the island in 1919. Cooper "developed a plan for using the tides to generate electric power, through the construction of a system of dams and sea-gates and the creation of two great basins, one in Passamaquoddy Bay and one in Maine's Cobscook Bay. When the moon's pull is strongest, the tides at the head of the Bay of Fundy rise and fall as much as fifty-three feet. In 1935, Roosevelt allocated ten million dollars in relief funds to the project and sent three thousand relief workers to prepare the site, but the effort had to be abandoned a year later when Congress refused to advance further funds. The plan was opposed by Canadian fishing interests and rejected by the United States engineers as too remote and expensive."[9]

However, since the price of oil has risen so much in recent years and its availability has slackened, there is renewed interest in the possibility. Although its construction would be expensive (over $500 million) and operating and maintenance costs would be high (over $30 million per year), there would be no fuel costs, unlike fossil-fuel-fired or nuclear plants. Proponents say it would recoup its initial cost and become a clean, inexpensive yearly source of over 250 million watts of electricity.

Only time will tell which of those two energy project proposals, if either, will eventually be constructed. Both have the potential to alter the area and the lives of its residents drastically, for better or worse.

One project which already has altered the lives of Campobello islanders was the opening of a bridge linking the island to Lubec, Maine, in 1962. Some residents felt that by ending their isolation from the rest of the world it took away part of their feeling of self-sufficiency and independence. Many residents complained, "We aren't an island anymore," but the bridge and the opening of the Roosevelt Park two years later brought additional jobs and income to Campobello, whose residents had previously relied almost solely on the whims of the sea to provide their livelihood.

Yet, when the park closes and the tourists leave in mid-October, the sense of being alone on an island returns. The two seasonal motels on the island shutter their doors for the winter along with their adjoining restaurants and several roadside fried-fish, pizza, and hamburger stands. There are no theaters, no nightclubs, no museums, and no shopping centers; just two general stores.

Entertainment other than Canadian television is provided by local initiative: the senior citizens' club holds dinners and quilting parties; the Canadian Legion Hall provides a place to drink alcohol, to dance, and to play pool, cards, darts, and bingo; and the island's consolidated high school and grade school sponsors sporting and other events. Most islanders have cars and the bridge allows them to come and go as they please, but other forms of entertainment are many miles away.

The fact that there are no bars or taverns on Campobello

(just two seasonal restaurants and the Canadian Legion Hall are licensed to serve liquor) reflects the island's long-standing tradition of teetotaling and the strong influence of religion on residents. Yet they have not always been uninvolved with alcoholic beverages.

During the economic hard times of the 1870s, islanders alleviated their financial plight by starting a new industry: rum running. "There were two warehouses on the island where not only rum but Holland gin, Irish and Scotch whiskies and French wines were kept in bond until they could be sold and taken aboard the fishing schooners that came up from Gloucester in fleets of thirty or forty ostensibly to buy herring."[10]

Outraged by the rum running in the Passamaquoddy Bay area, temperance societies and law-and-order leagues in several American and Canadian towns occasionally "forced reluctant officers to act. Usually such efforts were not very well coordinated and there was likely to be at least one 'oasis.' The *Eastport Sentinel* (February 25, 1880) reminded its readers now and then that Campobello was a 'rum' parish. During strict periods of enforcement considerable ingenuity was shown by thirsty Eastporters. The *Sentinel* (June 2, 1880) revealed that, 'among the latest discoveries in the shape of a device for smuggling is the tin bustle, manufactured for an Eastport female for the above purpose. It was filled but not in position when discovered.' "[11]

A similar situation occurred during the Prohibition Era of the 1920s. "Elderly Campobello fishermen tend to change the subject when asked about the rum running days when Black Diamond rum could be bought in Jamaica for seventeen cents for a five-gallon-keg that could be sold in the United States for $40, and Campobello fishermen would go out in their small boats to pick up liquor from the schooners anchored near The Wolves (islands) and carry it to Eastport or Lubec."[12]

Shown in an aerial photograph of the northern end of the island, Wilson's Beach is one of three communities on Campobello. It is home to Waldo and Margaret Mathews, who have lived in their attractive home for more than fifty years.

14

Says Waldo, "When the garden's in, every day somebody stops to take a picture. One feller stopped one day and leaned over the fence. After awhile I got him in. Well, he says, 'I'm gonna tell you something, now. This is my fourteenth year I've stopped and looked at your garden.' "

Waldo remembers that another visitor once told him, "I dread to go home where I live in New York. You people here are just as gentle and nice as can be; gettin' along lovely. We might go on the street in New York and somebody would shoot us, or knock us down, and take what money we had."

Other forms of smuggling prospered in the area at various times. During the Napoleonic War, at the beginning of the nineteenth century, Britain blockaded the entire continent of Europe, thus cutting off the United States. In retaliation Congress passed the Embargo Act in 1807 forbidding American ships to embark for any foreign port. Two years later Congress substituted the Non-Intercourse Act, which allowed American ships to trade with any country except England and France.

"Quickly Eastport, Maine, only two miles from Campobello, became one of the busiest towns in the United States. Smuggling became Campobello's chief industry. The islanders said, 'That's why fogs were made.' "[13]

Of course smuggling wasn't a continuous occupation for the islanders' forefathers, who not only fished but also farmed and occasionally worked as loggers or mill hands. Today's approximately twelve hundred island residents live in three scattered communities (at North Road, Welshpool, and Wilson's Beach) centered around the Harbour de L'Outre on the nine-mile-long island's protected western side. Most of the islanders work as fishermen or fish processors. Some specialize in one of many types of fishing such as hand-lining, lobstering, trawling, dragging, gillnetting, seining, or weir tending. Others do a little bit of several kinds of fishing. Some residents, especially those living at Welshpool near the former summer colony and Roosevelt Park, make their living keeping shop or catering to tourists in season. Others work at the sardine-canning factory located at Wilson's Beach. A few build boats, repair automobiles, or do odd jobs, such as carpentry. In the fall some men and quite a few women and children go "tipping" to gather evergreen boughs from which they fashion Christmas wreaths.

There is a twine shop at Welshpool that employs several

people to make and repair nets for the fishing boats, although many nets are repaired right on the wharves where the boats are tethered.

Whatever they do, the people of Campobello do it with little or no sense of urgency. They take their time and enjoy their lives, whether or not they happen to enjoy the particular task at hand. Maybe they are attuned to the rhythmic changes of the tide or the seasons. Even in the sardine factory, where women are prodded by the incessant demands of a nonstop conveyor belt loaded with herring to process, there are smiles and friendly snatches of conversation to be caught. Although paid for piecework, they take time to stop and talk with strangers, to laugh and gossip.

Their speech is easily recognizable. They talk, "with an accent distinctly different from that of either the nearby Canadian islands of Deer Island and Grand Manan or the neighboring Maine coast. Their speech with its broad 'a,' slurred 'r' and such intonations as might come from the mouth of a Frenchman who had learned his English in Wales, is much the same as that of their eighteenth-century ancestors. A native of Campobello could recognize another anywhere as soon as he heard him speak."

Shortly after being exposed to their unique accent and some of the interesting accounts related by islanders, I decided to tape-record conversations with several people. In that way I could supplement my own impressions of the island and what I had read and related of her history with the thoughts and words of some of her own people, without any intermediary.

Two of the conversations I transcribed are with transplanted residents who talk about their quests to be accepted by the communities into which they moved fifteen and thirty years ago, respectively. Two other conversations are with elderly islanders. One was the oldest man living on Campobello. The other is a lady who refuses to grow old. They both tell what it was like living on the island for the past eighty to ninety years. One resident tells part of the story of his life in verse. Another, the last surviving former employee of the Roosevelt family, tells what it was like working in the summer home of the president of the United States. Finally, a now-deceased Lubec resident and former naturalist for the Roosevelt Park describes the ecology of the island.

Aside from those conversations, there are some fascinating stories about Campobello and her past which can be read from several sources (see bibliography). It is not my intention to duplicate extensively what has been written or said before about Campobello and her interesting history. Others have told it better and more completely than I can in the space and time available here. Rather

I prefer to just introduce the island by way of the previous narrative and try to establish a feeling for her that has grown steadily during more than one hundred days I have spent there since October 1975. I hope that the pictures contained herein and the recorded words of her people will best describe what I found and love about Campobello.

STEPHEN O. MUSKIE
June 1982

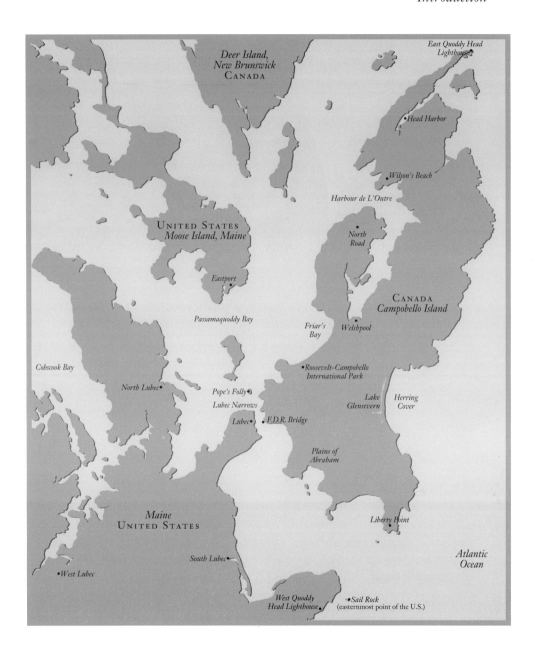

Deer Island,
New Brunswick
CANADA

East Quoddy Head
Lighthouse

•Head Harbor

•Wilson's Beach

Harbour de L'Outre

UNITED STATES
Moose Island, Maine

North
Road

Eastport

Passamaquoddy Bay

CANADA
Campobello Island

Friar's
Bay

Welshpool

Cobscook Bay

•Roosevelt-Campobello
International Park

North Lubec•

Pope's Folly•

Lubec Narrows

Lake
Glensevern

Herring
Cover

Lubec• •F.D.R. Bridge

Plains of
Abraham

Maine
UNITED STATES

Liberty Point

Atlantic
Ocean

South Lubec•

•West Lubec

West Quoddy
Head Lighthouse•

•Sail Rock
(easternmost point of the U.S.)

Linnea Calder, now the Roosevelt Campobello International Park's historical consultant, grew up in the Campobello world of the Roosevelts where she and her parents worked.

LINNEA CALDER

Historian Consultant for the

Roosevelt Campobello International Park

FDR's home on Campobello is the main attraction to more than 130 thousand visitors who yearly tour the Roosevelt Campobello Park, established in 1964 as the world's first international park, jointly funded and operated by the United States and Canada.

Encompassing some twenty-six hundred acres, or most of the southern end of the island, the park is open to visitors seven days a week from the end of May until the middle of October.

Most visitors arrive in private cars, but tour buses account for about eight thousand of the tourists, who come from every state in the United States, every province in Canada, and several foreign countries.

Besides Franklin D. Roosevelt's former summer home, the park consists of four other restored cottages from the summer colony era, a visitors' center, and a "natural area," traversed by several hiking trails and two automobile drives.

Visitors can stroll casually through the thirty-four-room FDR "cottage," which was built "of that comfortably uncertain architectural style common to another era when people had money, sought room to spread out and eschewed formality (at least for the summer)."[16]

In the visitors' center two beautiful thirty-minute films, shown hourly, depict some of Campobello's history and President Roosevelt's relation to the place he called his "beloved island."

Other than the Roosevelt house and the visitors' center, the only other building regularly open to the public is the restored Hubbard cottage, which can be toured whenever there are no conference groups using its facilities.

Nonprofit, international governmental, educational, scientific, and medical groups regularly use the park's facilities as a meeting place. In the past the New Brunswick Departments of Agriculture, Commerce and Development, Justice, and Tourism have held conferences on Campobello Island along with American conference groups from the Maine Medical Center, the University of Maine's Canadian-American Center, and the International Conference of Human Rights and Peace.

"A lot of people come back every year just to see the spectacular flower gardens," says assistant park superintendent Galen Sheehan, continuing, "They love the way the grounds and cottages are kept and how friendly our personnel are."

Yet, the average visitor doesn't spend much time at the park. "They run right in from Lubec, see both movies, spend a half hour at the Roosevelt house, and a half hour at the Hubbard house. Everybody's in a hurry. They seem to think they are slowing down on their vacation, but they're not, really. They beam right in here and beam right out again," says Galen. Only about five or ten percent spend any time in the natural area, one of the highlights of the park.

Linnea Calder, the Roosevelt Park's historian consultant, grew up in the Campobello world of the Roosevelts for whom she and her parents worked. She is often available at the visitors' center or the FDR cottage to answer questions posed by curious visitors. Here she relates some of her memories of childhood and later years:

"I'll be seventy-one in May 1982.

"The earliest age that I remember going to the FDR house was when I was just small. My father was still alive. He was care-taker there. He died when I was six years old. I have several memories of being there with him. It was before I was six years old that I first went to the house.

"I don't know how long my father was caretaker there. I think it was for a long time. I know he even visited Hyde Park. Also, he helped build the swimming pool, the one that's been filled in down here.

"My mother probably wasn't working in the house, but she started as laundress. Someone was in the house one time making a fuss over me and one of the guards said, 'I don't see what they're making such a fuss over her for. Her mother was only the laun-dress.' Franklin Jr. was quite put out when he heard it. He said, 'She was much more than the laundress, before she finished work-ing.' At the time I said, 'Yes, she was laundress and I'm not ashamed of it. She made an honest living.'

"I remember Johnny was quite small. He was either in his nurse's arms or in a carriage and I went over to speak to him, like a child would. My father called me back and said that I shouldn't go over and the nurse said that was all right; to let me come over.

"They had four boys and a girl, except there was a boy who died in infancy. Anna was the oldest. Anna's dead and Johnny's dead; the oldest and the youngest. The other children are Franklin, James and Elliott.

"After working as a laundress, my mother was a house-

Two visitors pause to take a photograph of the Roosevelt cottage from an especially good vantage point. More than 130 thousand people visit the park yearly, arriving mostly by private automobile from every state in the United States and every province in Canada as well as many foreign countries. ◄

Watching the sun set across Passamaquoddy Bay, Harry and Judy Stevens gaze through the oval window of the Hubbard cottage, one of four restored turn-of-the-century houses at the Roosevelt Park, of which Harry is the superintendent. ▶

keeper, I suppose, would be what you'd call it, starting in 1926. She was the housekeeper for both cottages, Mrs. James (Granny) Roosevelt's and Franklin's. She had to see to the cleaning and opening of them and have supplies in when the family came.

"Granny's cottage was torn down in 1949 or 1950; maybe it took two years to get it all down. Elliott had acquired the property. At least he had power of attorney. He and Mrs. Roosevelt had formed Roosevelt Enterprises. He was in charge of all the properties, I guess. He decided they wouldn't be using two houses. The one house, the Franklin house, would be sufficient for the family if they wanted to come up in the summer. Since the family wasn't coming as much as they used to they wouldn't need two cottages. On account of taxes; on account of the water situation; on account of the closeness of the two cottages and because it needed a lot of repair work done on it, he decided that he would rather have it torn down.

"It is too bad, but James told me that he never understood why Elliott had the house torn down 'til he talked with Elliott and Teddy, my son who tore the house down. James said then he understood the reason for tearing it down and he would have agreed with it.

"I helped clean Granny's house many times. It was similar in style to Franklin's, but smaller. In a way, you could call it a nicer house. It was more compact; more like a home. Whereas the Roosevelt cottage is like a summer home. I liked both of them, but I liked Franklin's house the best, anyway.

"Franklin was given this house when he married Eleanor, a few years after they were married. Granny gave him his house. It was built in 1897 for a family by the name of Kuhn, from Massachusetts. Their name is still on some of the furniture in the

Franklin house. The husband and the son died, and the widow, at her death, stipulated in her will that Mrs. James Roosevelt should have the first refusal on the house if she wanted to buy it. But if she did buy it she wanted her to give it to Franklin. She was very fond of Franklin. Granny Roosevelt bought it. We've never been able to ascertain the exact year, but we think it was something around 1909. She bought it so that his family would have their own summer home. They were married in 1905, March the 17th. She bought it a few years after. They called it a belated wedding gift.

"I think they spent summers at the Granny Roosevelt house [before obtaining their own house]. I really don't remember that much, but I assume they did, or parts of the summer anyway.

"I think it was 1923 or 1924, probably '24 that I started working there. My mother was doing the laundry at that time. I just did light things. Of course I was only twelve years old. In late years I've thought that Mrs. Roosevelt just made a job for me because I realize now that she had plenty of help and all I did was light dusting and empty waste paper baskets. There was a cook, a kitchen maid, another maid, and a butler, I think, besides a nurse. There were four or five on the staff in all.

"I remember Mrs. Roosevelt taking me into the kitchen and telling them, 'This is Linnea,' and what I was going to do and for them to have a glass of milk and a sandwich, or a piece of cake, or some cookies, or something for me.

"My mother wasn't in the house at the time. She did the laundry work out at her place. They used the laundry room in the house more for the children's things and for personal laundry.

"In 1921 FDR contracted polio. That was before I started work there. I really haven't any memory of him at Campobello except vaguely. It's one of those things, do I remember or do I just

28

Meticulously groomed, colorful flower gardens are a major attraction at the Roosevelt Park. They grace the front lawn of the Prince cottage, the Visitors' Center, and the other buildings clustered around the FDR cottage on the fifty-acre main compound of the park.

remember from hearing people tell of it, you know, and seeing pictures. I can remember being there with my father and seeing a man who, I presume, was Roosevelt walking around the grounds, or talking with my father.

"I remember having conversations with Mrs. Roosevelt, but not with the president.

"The whole family continued to go up there after 1921 sometimes, and then, as Anna and the two older boys grew older, they grew away from the place. They still would come back occasionally, but they didn't come the way they did previously. Sometimes Mrs. Franklin would come up and bring Johnny and Franklin, but they gradually grew away from the place, too. All of the summer people, the younger generation, did, too. The style of life changed and there wasn't life enough up around here for them.

"They would come usually around the first of July, maybe the end of June, and they would leave in September in time to go back when schools opened. They were there for the whole summer.

"I think Elliott and I are the same age; there's a few months' difference. I don't ever remember talking with or playing with any of the Roosevelt children, but I can remember Elliott, one summer when I was working there. He and I disagree on what summer it was. I remember that he and James had been on a trip out west and he came to Campobello when they came back. The rest of the family was up here. I can remember, he was tall, and blond-headed, very attractive. I helped unpack his suitcase and get his things put away in his bedroom.

"The summer colony kept to itself a great deal. There were the Porters, Archer-Shees, Princes, Hubbards, the two Roosevelt houses, and the Shober house. There were three at Shobers, and two at Hubbards. There was quite a large family at the Prince cottage and the Archer-Shees family was quite large and they were all about the same age as the Roosevelts. Two or three of the Prince grandchildren were here last summer. They came and asked for me and I took them through the cottage and over to Shobers.

"There were two families or three families in Welshpool that were summer colony, too, and they had children, like the Pattersons and the Steels, from Baltimore, who had some young people. There was a boarding house, too, directly across from the post office in Welshpool and people used to come there to stay.

"The Roosevelts had a lot of bedrooms. They had friends of the children or relatives staying for short times or sometimes they probably came and stayed the summer. I remember that one summer Louis Howe's daughter was up. I remember her distinctly and it's been a long time. They always had someone visiting.

"Then there was the Adams family. Mrs. Adams was the president's cousin and there were two children over there, in those log cabins.

"The Archer-Shee cottage has been torn down; the Porter cottage is in the process of falling down. The Archer-Shee house was a large house; they were a large family from England. I think there were three boys and three girls, and they used to come over to the Roosevelts' a lot.

"Most of the changes on the island have been since the bridge came. There's a great difference in the life-style. People were poorer in those days, before the bridge was built. When Elliott was here in '67 or '68, he said it didn't seem like the same island to him. He said he drove over the island and there were beautiful homes here and each home had at least one car in the dooryard. It was just altogether different that way. Although people didn't have much before the bridge, they still owned their own land and their own home.

An aerial view of the Roosevelt Park's main compound shows all the buildings located within it, including (clockwise from top left) the Visitors' Center, Prince cottage and (below it) the administration building, the FDR cottage, the site of Granny Roosevelt's cottage, Hubbard cottage, Wells-Schober cottage and Johnston cottage. All the cottages were once part of the summer colony which developed at the turn of the century.

Linnea Calder

After being afflicted with polio, President Roosevelt was moved into a small, sparsely-furnished bedroom on the first floor of his summer house so that he wouldn't have to climb any stairs.

"After Elliott sold the house to the Hammer brothers in 1952, I continued working for the Hammers. Dr. Hammer said I was a walking encyclopedia on the Roosevelt family. They liked to have me there because if they had visitors who wanted any information I could get it to them, so I worked for them all the while they owned the house. When the two governments took the house over I continued on with them and I've been there all along.

"But, it wasn't continuous because I married and we had a grocery store. We supplied the Roosevelt families with groceries during the summer and my mother was working for them, so I was in contact with them all the time, but I wasn't really working for them until after my husband died and then I worked summers when they were here.

"My mother continued working for them. She continued going to Hyde Park for years. She was Mrs. Roosevelt's housekeeper in her apartment in New York after the president died. I don't know how long she worked. She had to stop because her sister became ill here on the island and she had to come home and stay with her. I think that was some time in the 1950s. When my mother died in 1955, someone who had interviewed her said she had worked for the Roosevelt family forty years.

"She helped close up the house for the Roosevelts. She told me when we were packing things in 1952, 'Linnea, do you realize this is the fifth house I have helped close for the Roosevelt family.' She had helped close the two New York houses, the Hyde Park house, Granny Roosevelt's house here, and she was closing this house.

"I said that my mother was jack-of-all-trades and master of none and I guess that's what I was, too. While Elliott owned the house, from 1947 or '48 until '52 when he sold it, I was caretaker of the house, and I was caretaker for the Hammers for several years. I did everything and anything that needed to be done. When they came they wouldn't have any guests with them or anything. Either my mother or I would be there to take care of them. Sometimes, if they came up to stay for a longer interval, they would bring one of the girls up from Hyde Park, or Mrs. Roosevelt's girl from the Stone cottage. Sometimes I cooked for them.

"I've kept in touch with the family since they stopped coming regularly. I have Christmas cards from some of them, and Franklin always is in contact. I was at Mrs. Roosevelt's funeral and at the ceremonies they had in Lincoln Center for Mrs. Roosevelt in 1962.

"I was often in touch with Johnny while he lived, but with Franklin more than any of them. Johnny used to come while the Hammers had the house. He was friends with them, and he was a guest of theirs many times. The family didn't come back after the house was sold until it became the park. James, Elliott, Franklin, and Johnny were here for a family reunion in 1979, I think it was. Some of the grandchildren were here, too.

"The Hammers didn't change the house very much. Elliott and Johnny had come here before they sold the house and they took a lot of things away, but when the Hammers bought it, they brought most of the things back. If they brought any different furnishings or furniture, it was still Roosevelt items that they had purchased from other Roosevelt homes. They bought a lot of the Roosevelt furniture and artifacts, and the only thing that's been really changed in the house is the curtains and the bedspreads. There is a slightly different arrangement of furniture in some of the rooms. That has been done so the public can view the furniture.

"I don't know of anything that the Hammers kept for sentimental reasons. A lot of things were brought here [from the Hammer Gallery] and turned over with the house, like the presidential flags and the president's chair and different things like that.

"When I started working at the park, at first I was over in the house as a guide. But, still, I was the one who opened the house and closed it. Now I don't do any of that. From 1967 I was in the visitors' center. I was there when the Queen Mother visited, but I also gave her a tour through the house. I was senior receptionist up until a few years ago. I was also the head housekeeper for all the houses, in charge of supplies and seeing that they were ready if anyone came to stay. Now, for three or four years I've been historian consultant. Before, I worked through the winter. Now I'm only on call [in the winter].

"I was at Hyde park one winter in 1926 and '27 with my mother. Until Christmas we stayed in the Stone cottage at Val-Kill and then we went over to the big house. Val-Kill [named after a stream that runs through the property] is a few miles from the big house. I was going to school, but I helped my mother evenings and Saturdays. I was fifteen then. I didn't like Hyde Park. It was too far from Campobello. No water there; no ocean. You can jump across the Hudson.

"I've been back dozens of times. I was there for Granny Roosevelt's funeral and several years ago to the memorial celebration. Franklin had me come up. I was there with the tour from the park two years ago. I've been there a couple of times separate from that, such as when the king and queen were there in '39. Mrs. Roosevelt took me up to be presented to them. The queen shook hands with us, but, of course, the king didn't.

"I could write a book about odd things that have happened at the park. There was a woman who came in one day. She came

Centerpiece of the Roosevelt Park, the thirty-four-room FDR cottage is open to visitors each day from late May through mid-October. About 1909 Franklin and Eleanor Roosevelt received the cottage as a belated wedding gift from his mother, who lived in the house next door.

➤ *Other than FDR's home, the only Roosevelt Park cottage regularly open to the public is the Hubbard cottage, which can be toured any time there isn't an international conference group using its facilities.*

◀ *Two park visitors relax and enjoy the solitude and beauty of the park's gardens near the site of the cottage owned by James and Sara Roosevelt. Also known as the Granny Roosevelt cottage, it was torn down by the Roosevelt family about 1950.*

◀ *Perched atop Friar's Head is a viewing platform, the highest point on Campobello, from which can be seen a 360-degree panorama of the area surrounding the island. It is equipped with binoculars and displays which identify landmarks of interest to park visitors.*

through the door of the visitors' center and she said, 'How in the name of God did he ever find his way to this God-forsaken hole?' I just stood there and looked at her and said, 'Lady, he must have loved it here because he came each summer and we also love it. We think it's a beautiful island.' She got angry at me.

"Another time, I was over in the house. I went on a coffee break and when I came back there was a man standing in front of the president's bedroom just looking in. I said, 'President Roosevelt occupied that bedroom in 1933.' He just turned and looked at me. I said, 'Really, he did. I worked here and I know.' He said, 'I couldn't care less!' I said, 'Well, I'm sorry. If you feel that way why did you bother to come in?' A lady spoke up from over in the museum end and she said, 'I'll tell you why. Everything that's gone wrong in the last hundred years he blames on Roosevelt.' I said, 'It's plain to be seen, one of you is a Republican and the other is a Democrat.' She laughed, but he didn't.

"In 1933 the secret service chose that downstairs area [where the man mentioned above had been standing] for the president because the museum had been fixed up as a reception room and office and there was a bedroom there that the secret service used as an office. Then, of course, there was that bedroom for him with the porch outside. He could go out without having to go up and down stairs. There was a bathroom right across the hall so the whole unit was sort of self-contained. He wouldn't have to be carried up and down stairs.

"He didn't have a wheel chair here. We didn't have any ramps or anything. They carried him in the litter and, I think, one time they just carried him out in a chair. He was just out on the lawn in front of the front door. I think he was just in one of the wicker chairs.

41

"I only saw him carried on the litter once I guess. He was here for about three days in 1933. They carried him down to the beach on it and they probably carried him around the grounds on it times when I was working and wasn't watching. They could have used it in '36 to carry him up from the beach. My husband helped carry him up.

"He came back three times: in '33, '36, and '39. I think he was here about three days in '33. In '36 I wasn't working in the house; I think he was just here over night. I was in the house to see him, but I wasn't working. In '39 I believe he came in the morning and left in the afternoon. I saw him, spoke with him, and took groceries up to the house. I think he was just here the one day.

"I had the grocery store and delivered groceries up to the house. I went there in the morning just after he came and the secret service wouldn't let me in then. I said, 'OK, if I go home and get a loaf of bread and come back, will you let me in to deliver the bread?' They let me in. They found out that I could go in."

Mazie Mathews proudly displays photographs of herself riding on her son's snowmobile. Although she is over eighty years old, she insists that her age will not prevent her from enjoying things she wants to do.

MAZIE MATHEWS

MAZIE MATHEWS repeatedly told me, "I'm not gonna get old." And, as if to prove it, she pointed with pride to photographs and newspaper clippings showing herself riding her son's snowmobile the previous winter. She is an avid devotee of quiltmaking and rarely misses an opportunity to gather with her friends at the senior citizens' club where they fashion one quilt after another. She also makes aprons and potholders which she prefers to give away rather than sell.

"I was born right here on this island, in a little white house up there on the side of the road," Mazie recalls. "My husband, Archie, and I have lived in this house since the kids were small. I s'pose we been here thirty years, I'll bet.

"Now that I'm over eighty, they won't let me stay here in the winter since Archie died. Now, I gotta go with Carrie Pearl, my daughter. I went out and stayed with her last winter. She's got a nice trailer out past the cemetery.

"It was a lot different growing up when I was a girl than it is now. But we had fun just the same. We was taught different. All of our toys and everything was put away when it came Saturday night. And they weren't touched. No bicycles, no sleds, no nothing. But, boy, it's different now. Course, now, most of the parents are out working. And that makes a difference. You can't take care of your house and the children if you're away working.

"There wasn't no liquor those days, when I was younger, around here. There was no dope and the mess there is now. And it seems awful funny cause I never seen it or heard tell of it. The kids around home, they didn't have any liquor.

"Archie went to school up to the other end of the island. Ours was down here. We used to go skating and sliding and that's where I first met him.

"We'd slide down over the hills in the winter time. No cars to bother us. Oh, we had a picnic. And when we skated, we went to Mill Cove. There was a pond out there. Wasn't a very big one, but it was lovely. We enjoyed it all together. Had a barrel of fun.

"When night came we didn't stay out too long. We was warned not to stay out too long. The boys would go home with us. Just go to the door. That's as far as they could go.

"Oh, one night, I remember, there was Bertie Brown and I. We both had boyfriends. Bertie had Clarence Newman. We called him Dewey. 'He's going to take me home tonight,' she said. I said, 'Well, Tom Brown's going to take me home tonight.' So, after we got through skating, we started home. Tom came to his house first before he did mine. He said, 'Goodnight,' and I went the rest of the way alone. Oh, they had a barrel of fun over that. Tom never went home with Mazie again.

"They called us, 'Bobby Town,' and we called them, 'Sou' Wackers.' Just for fun I s'pose. They'd walk down here from the Pool and we'd walk up there. We didn't think it was very far. Where our senior citizens' hall is now, they'd have dances there, and they used to have box suppers and dramas. They used to do it for people that needed money. Of course, when they had dances the music was right from home.

"I think the [nicknames for people on the island] are dreadful. I don't like nicknames. I was talkin' about Dewey. His name was Clarence Newman. They always called him Dewey Newman. Too lazy to speak the right name, I think. Sometimes they'll say Flora-Dewey, like that, for his wife. Emma-Horace; they all said that, too. Oh, so many names like that. That's silly. They always said Sadie-Leslie. She's gone. Now Leslie lives up there alone. June and Buster. Now her name is June and his is Winston. That sounds silly too. I don't like those nicknames. Bessie and Jack Fitzgerald: Bessie-Jack. I don't know why they say that. I never wanted them to say Mazie-Archie and they never did.

"I've made quilts for I don't know how long. I've got a bedroom full up there that's gotta be quilted. And some, they're lovely. They're beautiful. And I make a lot of pot holders. I don't want to sell them. I give most of them away. A girl from St. Andrews called me; said she wanted three dozen. I only charged a quarter for each one. I hate to do that. I'd rather give them to anybody.

"There was so many who had quilts to make and lots of people don't have homes large enough to do them. So, we decided we'd take one room up to the church just for ourselves. That was a long time ago. People that's got quilts that wants them done, we put our names down. I think I've got thirty now on the list. There's one in now, but as a rule we have two there to work on. And that's the way they do it. They bring it there with the back, the lining, and the thread. All we have to do is put 'em in the frames. Then we take an afternoon or whenever we want. As a rule we quilt on Tuesday. Lots of times we stay there evenings, too. Take a little lunch; have coffee and tea.

"I never touched fish and never would. I didn't ever tell nobody why I didn't like fish. I don't want anyone else to get turned off to it. It's something that happened. That was in 1932 and I have never eaten a piece of fish since.

"I don't like fish and I'm scared of water. One thing I did do. Over on Casco Bay Island there was barrels and barrels of cranberries that grew there. They was the marsh cranberries. The big ones. So, one day, Archie said, 'Let's go over to Casco Bay Island and pick some cranberries. It was nice and calm. He took a pillowcase and they had this thing to rake the berries with and we got a pillowcaseful. Of course, our grandchildren had a barrel of fun. Archie took us over in a rowboat. I didn't know what we was going in. Course the men thought a rowboat was all right cause they'd used lots of 'em.

"Wasn't I scared going over. I can see the grandchildren now. Doubling right up and laughin' at Nana cause she was scared. When I got on that island, I said, 'I'm not going back home, Archie.' He said, 'Woman, you've gotta go back home. You can't stay here all night. Whatcha talkin' about? If I went home without you I'd be killed.' I thought. I declared I wasn't gonna get in that rowboat again. But I had to get in it. It was only the tide, I guess, that was rough. Archie said it was the way the tide was going. They didn't think it was rough, but I thought it was awful. I've never been in a rowboat since. Nothin' doin' in a boat.

"I've never had any desire to live anywhere else. Just cause it's home I guess. I'd rather be here than anywhere else. Now, it's lovely to St. John. I was up there this winter and stayed two months. But the best part of my visit was coming home."

ASA BROWN

UNTIL he moved to neighboring Deer Island a couple years ago, Asa Brown, at ninety-three, was Campobello's oldest resident. He is still its "most renowned talker, but on the page his words are like the lyrics of a song without the music. Like all the islanders, his speech depends to an extraordinary degree on timing, intonation, facial expression, gesture and, most subtly of all, on implication: what is said is often less meaningful than what is deliberately left unsaid."[15]

Several other people I interviewed mentioned Asa and had stories to tell about him. Bud Mitchell recalled that "The tourists come here talkin' to Ace one time and asked him how old he was. 'Well,' he says, 'I'm eighty-five.' They said, 'What do you owe it to fer living so long?' Well, Ace says, 'I'll tell ya. I never smoked 'til I was nine year old. An I never touched alcohol in any way, shape nor form 'til I was twelve. An I been smokin' and drinkin' ever since.'"

Mazie Mathews says that after Asa's wife died, his sons asked him to go live with them on Deer Island, but Asa told them, "I've set in this chair for ninety years. I'm gonna sit here the rest of the time." However, he finally gave in to their requests, but hopefully, for the rest of us, he will carry on the tradition of his story telling.

Asa's recollections blend easily with his acute observations on human nature: "My grandfather, well, he was a fisherman; he was a boatbuilder, a sailmaker, he was a jack-of-all trades, he could do any damn thing. He used to make masts for all the boats. They used to bring the big things here from Grand Manan and upshore for him to make masts for them boats, and he made sails for 'em. Lots of 'em. They had a building right down here with a fish house underneath and upstairs he built boats. They used to build dories and dinghies, or any damn thing anybody wanted, and he used to go around those years caulking vessels. He was all the time doing something. He never lost no time.

"You might say, and you know it has to be, everybody on this island, and the first of 'em, they're all foreigners, wasn't they? They didn't come from here cause there was no one here to have them, was there? They come from some other country. My grandfather, my mother's father, come from Ireland. And my other grandfather, he come up on the St. John River. I don't know, I forget just why. Anyway, he come here in a log canoe. Come with his father. And they're all the same.

"I think the tourists are a wonderful thing. Course, some people don't. I'll tell you the reason they don't. Now this world, and you know just as well as I do, this world is nothin' but money. It don't make a damn bit of difference how you get it or where you get it.

"There's people here don't get no money out of the tourists. They say, 'Them damn things takin' all the highway road. You come down on one of the breakwaters. The breakwater's full of cars. Them damn things fishin'. Never spend a cent.' While there's other people who's gettin' a lot of money out of 'em, and they say

Well into his nineties, Asa Brown was Campobello's oldest resident, until he recently moved to neighboring Deer Island.

49

it's lovely. And that's just what I tell 'em. I say, 'You're jealous. Yes, you're only jealous because you ain't gettin' no money out of 'em.' And it's the truth.

"Money is the ruination of this world; in one sense of the word. Look at people today. Goddamn it, they'd murder me or you or anyone to take a chance; no difference whether you got any money or not. They'd murder you to search you. See if you did have any money. And if you haven't got no money out amongst that crowd of people you ain't noticed very much are you? No.

"And you don't have very much to say. This here running the country. They say, 'Well, why don't you say something?' What the hell would be the good of me to say how the country was run? Well, they'd laugh at you, say, 'Well, that damn, ignorant fool up there doesn't know what he's talkin' about.'

"It's just like these fish inspectors. I've forgotten more puttin' my boots on than any one of them knows about fish. They don't know no more about takin' care of a fish than I would about running an airplane. Not a damn bit more.

"I see one here last summer. Hired as a government inspector. Well, she was a girl. She was talkin' to me down on the wharf. Every day I'd have a yarn with her. I talk to everybody. One day she come to me and she says, 'Mr. Brown, what's them fish in there with the yellow specks on 'em.' I said, 'Them's codfish.' She said, 'How do you know?' I said, 'You can tell by lookin' at 'em. Look at the spots on 'em; freckles on 'em. She said, 'I thought they's hake.'

"Here from the government, mind you; inspectin' fish. I guess she was about eighteen. College girl. Half of them they send down, that's what they are: college students. Send them down here and they tell us how to catch fish and what to do with them.

"People down there, tourists, about every other one of 'em,

I don't know why, they come talk to me. One day I was comin' in. I had a string of herring, big herring. I was bringin' 'em home to cook. Had my old pipe, had an old crooked stem on it, in my mouth. Man and a woman stopped me, said, 'You're Mr. Brown?' I said, 'Well, I'm one of 'em, I s'pose.' Well, she said, 'I think you're the one we're lookin' for. We was down here about two weeks ago and you showed a friend of ours how to catch fish, and fixed their lines for 'em, and they told us when we come down first thing to do is inquire for you. What's the matter with takin' your picture before we go?'

"I said, 'Yes, I s'pose you can take a picture. I'll lay this old pipe down.' She said, 'No! Put that pipe right back in your mouth and hold them fish in that string!' I did. They sent me a picture, too. They send me pictures all the time, different ones that take my picture.

"I don't care nothin' about lobsters. I don't. My wife, she's crazy over lobsters. From the time I was big enough to see one, my father was off lobster fishing, and all of us had funny lobsters. I s'pose one reason is I didn't care nothin' about 'em count of just fishin' 'em or something. I don't know.

"I'd get some lobsters somewhere, set down to the table, and my wife would say, 'S'posing somebody come in the house. You eatin' bologna; me eatin' lobster.' I'd rather have the balogna, and that's the worst stuff ever made.

"Years ago, when I was growin' up, these stores, well that's where people went to loaf; all these old fellers. I used to be a kid. I'd go up to listen to the old fellers tell these yarns, you know. They all had chairs around. Had a big spittoon in the middle of the floor. Anybody wanted to could chew tobacco. Everybody fillin' up their pipes or smokin'. Wasn't interfering the customers cause they was away from the counter, you know. Ah, they stayed there all day and, well, about nine o'clock at night they'd close up. And there's where everybody used to go. All the old fellers. And us kids used to like to get in there and listen to 'em. Half the things they told us was things that happened to their neighbors. Didn't amount to much.

"Yes, everything's changed. When I was growin' up here . . . when I was a man, as far as that goes, if I ever was one . . . why, your neighbors used to come see you. There'd never be an evening there wouldn't be seven or eight people in here. Now, we never see nobody. Never a soul ever opens the door.

"Cars, now. That's the trouble. Any time we ain't got nothin' to do we take the old car and go to Lubec, or Calais, or St. Stephen, or somewhere. If we didn't have a car, there we'd be, settin' right here all day and all night, wouldn't we?

"First car owned on this island was owned by Harry Jackson. Side curtains on it. There was one here before that. There was a doctor come here and rented a house. Stayed here a year or so, and he had a car. First time it come down the road, kids were chasin' it, and even men. Thought it was a curio, which it was.

"We had telephones here quite awhile before we had electricity. Had telephones fifteen years, twenty years before we had electricity.

"When you look at it now you wonder how you lived [before modern conveniences]. And you didn't live. You just existed. You just stayed here. But you was all in the same boat. You was just as well off as the other feller and the other feller was just as well off as you. You was all neighbors and friendly and sociable. Course you didn't know nothin' about this life [we have today]. You wouldn't imagine it.

"Had an old kerosene lamp. Half the time that would smoke up so you couldn't find it. If you wanted a bucket of water, you had to take your bucket and go to the well somewheres. In the wintertime, you'd go to the well. Well would be froze up. Go home and get an axe. Go down and cut a little hole. Squeeze the bucket down and lots of times you'd have to take a dipper with you. Went in the woods and cut your own wood. Never was such a thing as a kerosene stove, or anything like that, or electric stove. Oh, it's a great life now. If you can afford it.

"You want to get up in the night, you just reach out over the side of the bed, snap a button, and she's all lit up. If you want to come downstairs, you come down and the fire's all a'going. If you want a drink of water, you go over there and turn the faucet. You want some hot water to wash yourself, you just turn the other faucet. Oh, it's wonderful. No gettin' over it. It's really wonderful.

"I've often thought that if some of the old people come back, I don't know but they'd go crazy. Just see all these gasoline boats, and all these fish houses and buildings all lit up and all these street lights. Now I'll tell you, it would be some surprise, wouldn't it? You couldn't imagine it, of course."

Proudly displaying her University of Maine diploma, Evelyn Morrell stands in front of her Welshpool home. Over seventy years old when it was awarded, she was that school's oldest graduate.

EVELYN MORRELL

Evelyn Morrell, together with her daughter, Joyce, lives in the house built more than 140 years ago by the island's third principal proprietary, Admiral William Fitzwilliam Owen. Because the house is too large for the two of them alone, and because they need the financial help to keep it up, they rent rooms to visitors during the tourist season. Unlike what any motel could hope to provide, the Owen house offers a cozy, relaxed, hospitable atmosphere in which one quickly feels at home on the island.

Now in her mid-seventies, Mrs. Morrell is the oldest student to graduate from the University of Maine. An eloquent storyteller, she explains what it was like moving to the island more than thirty years ago and how she and her family adjusted to life there.

"We came up and saw this house, and the day that we were supposed to call it off and decide it would be too much for us and we couldn't swing it because it was too big, too expensive, too this, that, and the other — that's the day we bought it. That's been almost thirty years ago. We had never been to Campobello before.

"My husband said he would never come in a house until he had the deed, proving the house belonged to him, and they held up the deed until November. So it was a terrible month to move to Campobello, but we did; we came here in November. You could scrape the frost off the walls. The first thing we had to do was take off doors and saw them so they would close. No doors would close. And my husband ripped up blankets and insulated around the doors to keep the draft out, because everything was crooked and uneven.

"Joyce was ten years old when we came here. She hated it. She thought she was buried in the woods. I was homesick, too, but I wouldn't let my husband know that I figured we had made a mistake. I wasn't going to admit it. I'd look out the front door and the scenery was so gloomy and so glum that I thought, 'Oh, isn't this awful.' It would get to the marrow of your bones, and I thought, 'But, I can never let Wayne know how I feel,' because, then, he was sixty-five when we came here. He had told me it would kill him; the transition would kill him. I said, 'It might kill you, but we're going to find the place we like.' After living here, he said he'd had the best ten years of his life. Before that, he just existed. When he came here, he lived. He loved it. He had retired when Joyce was in kindergarten because he was twenty-five years older than I.

"People looked at us at a distance for two years. Two years they just looked at us and sized us up and kept away.

"Electricity came to the island just two years before we moved here. When we moved here we had a lot of appliances and gadgets that people around here didn't have and one of the things Wayne brought was an electric grinder, for grinding an axe or knife or something, and he had it down in the cellar on a beam. Bertram Calder came up one day and he said, 'Mr. Morrell, I hear you have an electric grinder. I would pay you to grind this two-bitted axe.' Wayne said, 'I don't want any pay for it, Bertram, but I'd be glad to grind it for you.' So he took it down in the cellar and he ground it and did a good job and brought it up. Bertram was delighted. He said, 'Are you sure I can't pay you? What can I do for you?' Wayne

With her daughter, Joyce, Evelyn sits on the front-hall stairway of the Owen house, built more than one hundred forty years ago by the island's third principal proprietary, Admiral William Fitzwilliam Owen, whose picture hangs on the wall.

Evelyn's friends gather in her dining room to sew a quilt, one of many which she designed.

said, 'Well, someday you just bring me a fish, big enough to cut into steaks.'

"Days went by; weeks went by; months went by. We never thought about the fish again. One day the three of us were sitting at the table and we looked down to the road at the end of our driveway. The gate opened and a man came through. He seemed to have sort of a pack on his back. He got a little closer and I said, 'Why, Wayne, that's Bertram and he's got a man on his back. He must have a sick man.' He kept getting closer and closer and closer, and he got up to the rise in the driveway. 'Holy smokes, what's he dragging? Why, that's a fish on his back!' And he came to the back door. Did you ever see the ad for Scott's Emulsion? The fellow had a cod fish over his shoulder and the tail was dragging on the floor. Just what he looked like. Wayne went to the door and he said, 'Well, Bertram, what's this all about?' He said, 'Morrell, I thought I'd wait 'til I got a big one.'

"We'd been here just a few months. Later we had our own chickens and hen house, but, up to this point, we didn't. Mary Kelly lived down the road, just beyond our gate, second house on the left, with her husband, Heb, and his older sister, Liney Kelly. I guess they called her Liney 'cause her name was Caroline. And Mary had a few hens and she sold eggs. I used to go down and get these nice, big, brown eggs. Every time I went down Liney was sitting in the kitchen. She was an old lady in her eighties.

"I went down one day and Liney wasn't any place around and I said, 'Where's Liney?' I could see Mary looked kind of worried and she said, 'Well, Liney isn't well and she's taken to her bed.' Liney's room was right off the kitchen. She said, 'We're really worried about her.' Well, I said, 'Mary, if there's anything I can do, you will let me know.' She said, 'Thank you, Mrs. Morrell.' They

59

called me Mrs. Morrell in those days. And out I went.

"Of course, Wayne and I were struggling with the problems around the house. It was early afternoon. We'd just had our lunch and were sitting in the den. We had a fire going in the fireplace. We were on either side of the fireplace discussing what project we would attack next.

"I heard the back door open and close and I heard steps come down the hall. Mary put her head in the doorway, and you could see her eyes were red; she'd been crying. Before I could ask her anything, Wayne said, 'Mary, dear, is there anything wrong? Come in.' She says, 'There is Mr. Morrell. Liney passed away, and Mrs. Morrell said if I needed her I should come and get her. I want her to come down and lay her out.' I said, 'You want me to what?' She said, 'I want you to come down and lay her out.' I said, 'Why, Mary, I've never been around a dead person. I couldn't do that. I never could do that.' Remember, Wayne was twenty-five years older than me. 'Now,' he said, 'Mary, dear, you go on home. Don't you think another thing about this. My wife will come down and she would be delighted to lay out Liney.' She thanked him and out she went.

"I turned around and I said, 'Wayne, are you losing your mind? I couldn't do such a thing. No possible way could I ever do it.' He said, 'All right, let me explain it this way. We've only been here a few months. Now, you turn down this dear, old woman in trouble, and the whole island's going to know about it. Here's a chance to be a real woman. Go down, lay her out. Do it. Don't let me hear any more about it. Go!' And I went. When he said do something, you did it. There was no liberation in my life. I didn't want any.

"When I went down there I went in the kitchen door. Mary

wasn't around, but I heard her rummaging in drawers upstairs. There was a little pantry off the kitchen and I found a white enamel pan. There was a pink towel over the towel rack and I took that. I found a cake of Ivory soap and a wash cloth. Got some warm water and I went in and the old lady was still warm.

"She had just died. She wasn't scrawny or disease-ridden or anything. She'd been beautiful when she was young: plump and firm, beautiful, warm. She just wore out.

"I washed her all over, and I powdered her. By the time Mary came down, I said, 'Go get me some underwear and get her dressed.' I remember putting the old-fashioned bloomers on her with the elastics around the knees; an old-fashioned shirt with a little drawstring and long sleeves, you know. Cotton stockings. She brought down a purple serge dress and I put that on her, and I said, 'Now find me a little piece of black velvet ribbon.' I tied the black velvet ribbon around her neck with a little bow in the back, and then I put a string of white pearls over that. Her hair was like spun, white, angel hair that you put on Christmas trees, you know. I fixed her hair up and she looked beautiful.

"When I went down there, oh, I weighed about a thousand pounds. After I did the job, oh, I felt light as a feather. So I looked at her and I was pleased and I went out the back door. I did the job and there was no more I could do and I came home. Wayne met me at the back door. He always called me, 'hon.' I'm anything but honey, but that's what he did, he called me, 'hon.' He said, 'How'd you make out, hon?' Flippantly, I said, 'Really, there's nothing to it after you get started. Really, I could lay out a morgueful.' So that was the adventure of my life since I've been here. And he was right: everybody on the island knew it. They said, 'Can you imagine why she would go to that woman instead of going to a native?'

"I went to the funeral. Mary's husband, Heb, was in the room with his two brothers from Lubec. Not one of them came up to me and thanked me for what I had done; for laying out their sister. I couldn't imagine why they never thanked me. I didn't want any money. I didn't want a gift. I wanted thanks, but they never did it. Just as though I never existed. Twenty years went on and I often wondered why they never thanked me. One of the brothers' wives, whom I'd been friendly with over the years, came over to see me last summer and I mentioned this to her. She said, 'Evelyn, Mary never told anybody that you laid out the old lady. She wanted the credit herself. The island knew it, but she didn't let on to the family. At least she let them think that she was the major one in doing it.' "

The Reverend Francis Mabey stands at the entrance to the United Baptist Church of Wilson's Beach, where he has been pastor since he moved to Campobello Island more than eighteen years ago.

THE REVEREND

FRANCIS MABEY

REVEREND FRANCIS MABEY, who moved to Campobello eighteen years ago, is pastor of the United Baptist Church at Wilson's Beach. An easygoing, yet ebullient man, he also oversees the operation of a church-affiliated summer camp for Charlotte County, New Brunswick, youngsters, including children from Campobello who wish to attend. Besides the Baptist church at Wilson's Beach, there is another unaffiliated Baptist church on the North Road, both a Catholic and Anglican church at Welshpool, and a Pentecostal church at Wilson's Beach.

"I'll never forget it," he recalls, "I came here on a November, Wednesday night. Blustery and cold. It was a bitterly cold November night. Unusual really. And, of course, like everybody else who comes to Campobello for the first time, I had my time all fouled up.

"I walked in the church. Walked in the side door, the belfry door. Here was the door all fastened and all caulked so it couldn't be opened. Course I wasn't living here very long before I understood why that was. The wind in the winter is a prevailing northwest wind and that door faces right in that way and it will blow you right off the seats. I thought to myself, 'My sakes, what kind of an outfit am I getting myself involved with here?'

64

"It was such a casual thing. I came to talk to the deacons and wound up preaching in the church. I moved here on the sixteenth of February in 1964 and been here ever since.

"The islander doesn't take new residents seriously because they're used to people coming and going like the tide. It takes awhile before they're convinced you're going to stay.

"I was here five years. I remember it just as clearly as if it were yesterday. I used to have a habit, on Monday nights, after my young people's group, my teenage group. Rather than come right home, I'd go down to one of the local service stations that stayed open. I'd walk in and all the men would be standing around talking and kibbitzing about. I'd walk in, walk to the pop corner and take a bottle of pop and get a bag of chips. And just talk to different ones. Maybe half an hour. Maybe three-quarters of an hour. 'See ya later fellers.' Then I'd go home. I did that for a long time.

"One day one of my men came to me. He said, 'I guess you've arrived. I was down at Jackson Brothers' today and so-and-so came over to talk to me. Right in the middle of the conversation, he interrupted himself and he said, "You know, that Mabey is not a bad fellow, is he? He comes down by Earl's and talks to us and so on." I guess you've arrived.'

"I was here just five years, almost to the day.

"Then, we've had a problem here. I've tried to explain it to the Royal Canadian Mounted Police (RCMP). We've sort of been an afterthought to the politician. We've been an afterthought to the education department and to the policeman. Consequently, there's no respect for those authorities. For many years, when I first came here, there were many people who drove around here without driver's licenses. Never had a driver's license in their life, because Campobello has been a law unto itself for so many years. It's been just left to itself, and so it established its own standards of law.

"So many of these situations, like Campobello, Deer Island, Grand Manan, or country areas outside the cities, have been way stations for young ministers getting a start. Or seminary students who go there in the summer and then, maybe, go back every Sunday through the year. Consequently, they got the idea, 'They don't take us seriously. We're just a stepping stone for something greater for them.'

"And, again, why wouldn't there be resentment? The minister is no better then than the mountie who says, 'Well, when I get around to it I'll come.' Or the government agency which says, 'Well, if there's anything left over maybe we can give it to Campobello, or Deer Island, or Grand Manan.'

"But, I don't blame people, you see. If the establishment doesn't take them seriously, seriously enough to commit themselves to them, why should there be respect for them? Why should there be respect for the church, if the church doesn't take them seriously?

"The Baptist Church went into Newfoundland somewhere around twenty-five years ago. They built a little church on posts. It was a sort of comme ci, comme ça operation. One day they decided it was time they put a basement under the church. The pastor was working away, all alone, one day getting ready to put the basement under the church, when one of the locals came along. He stood there and he looked for awhile and scratched his head and said, 'Are you really planning on staying?'

"There was no foundation. The pastor understood right then what that comment meant. Hadn't taken them seriously. You build a place up on posts, that's a temporary thing. Are you not serious enough to come and build a foundation?

"It's important right now that out here on the road they've

built a home for the mounties. There will be a permanency. Then, I think, they'll realize a sense of respect for them. Right up until recently we've never known whether the mountie was going to be here come Monday morning or not.

"We're strange here in our habits on the road. You're driving along through Wilson's Beach and, all of a sudden, you have to stop because there's another car stopped in front of you and there's a car stopped the other way and they're talking. They don't want you to blow your horn at them. They'll move on when they're ready. So you're patient because you might see somebody, just the next car, that you want to talk to.

"It's hard for people off the island to understand the casualness. The frustration of tourists when they come here in the summer that they can't get in the bank, they can't get into anything from twelve until one. Even the bank is closed right up tight. Terribly frustrating for people off the island. That's the way we treat life, you see, 'It's noon time; let's go eat.'

"Here I've found a very much less formal group of people. On Prayer Meeting night, the men all come with a shirt and sweater. Consequently, I now go to Prayer Meeting in a shirt and sweater. I don't know where you'd find another Baptist minister, cause we're supposed to be very staid and straight-laced, who would go to Prayer Meeting in a shirt and sweater.

" 'Time and tide wait for no man.' If you're doing tide work, when the tide comes up you might as well go home. There's no sense standing there. 'Well, I've got another hour's work to do.' You can't do it until the tide goes back down again. Consequently, there's a completely different appreciation of time here. When the tide is right, you go. Never mind what you're doing. Never mind what you'd like to do or where you'd like to go. The tide is there.

Built by the island's third principal proprietary in 1855, St. Anne's Anglican Church looks little different today than it did when Admiral Owen worshipped there himself. The Reverend Stephen McCombe greets parishioners as they leave Sunday services. When he visited Campobello, President Roosevelt attended services at St. Anne's.

Your trawl has to be hauled. Your traps have to be pulled. 'If we don't go now, we're gonna miss the daylight seine.' It's not a matter of, 'Well, let's hang around another couple of hours and then go.' You go because you know that if you don't go you might as well stay home because you're gonna miss the tide. Whether it's the slack you want, the high you want, or the low you want. You go when the tide is going to be there.

"At the same time we treat time a little more casually, time also becomes more our master. If you went to work at 7:30 this morning because the tide was right, tomorrow morning you're going to go to work at 8:30, and then 9:30, and so on, so your appreciation of time is different. You have to do all you can while you have that time because when the tide goes or comes, whether you've got it finished or not, you're not going to finish it until the next tide.

"Everybody on this island is invited to weddings here. There are no formal invitations, usually, because everybody is related to everybody else. Where would you start? They usually have invitations printed and send them to people off the island. Usually, the Sunday before the wedding, the minister will announce that so-and-so's wedding is coming up and everybody's invited.

"I get so involved with funerals sometimes. With people who've been off the island for twenty-five, thirty, forty years, and they come back for a funeral. For mother's funeral or dad's funeral. And they don't know what to think of us when they get here, because they're used to the impersonal nature of a funeral and a funeral home in the big city.

"And all of a sudden they get back here and they go back to the old homestead. The casket is in the living room. And the door doesn't stop swinging. Somebody comes with a salad. Somebody comes with a potato scallop. Somebody comes with a pie, and everybody's stopping to say, 'Now, we've got a bed, if you need a bed, or we've got this, we've got that. Whatever we've got is yours; use it.'

"How many times people have come to me after it's all over to say how they forgot what it was like to live on Campobello. They had just forgotten because in their circumstances they don't know who lives in the apartment downstairs, or upstairs, or even next door. Here, if you stub your toe, everybody knows and everybody's concerned.

"It's a different way of life than so many people are used to today, and they're so much the poorer because of their way of life. Maybe they have more conveniences than we do, but our young people are closer to one another. Our older people are closer to one another.

"We are three distinct communities. If you be here long enough, you can tell even by the voice, diction, whether they're from North Road, or Welshpool, or Wilson's Beach. It's sort of a never-the-twain-shall-meet concept.

"The people at Welshpool always, by and large, have worked for the tourists. That's where all of the large homes were: the Roosevelts, the Coopers, and all those people. That's been their work.

"Whereas Wilson's Beach, for a long time, for want of a better way of expressing it, was a lot of tar-paper shacks on the bank. That was the concept. At Wilson's Beach the people worked at fishing, and you didn't make anything at fishing thirty years ago.

"Folks at Welshpool were having a regular salary come in from these folks who came, whereas the people at Wilson's Beach basically had nothing. You fished all day and if you got a dollar for your catch when you got back, never mind that you had two or three thousand in the bank. If you got a buck, or so, you did all right.

"Then North Road is sort of a throwback to both. There's sort of a rivalry there. I don't know whether it will ever be stemmed.

"Somebody suggested here a couple of years ago — one of the politicians; I don't know which one — that Campobello should be incorporated as a village. I said, 'That would be the worst thing in the world that you could do. Maybe it worked on Grand Manan; it won't work here. If you want to incorporate three villages, go ahead, but don't try to incorporate one village on Campobello, because it just won't work. We're three distinct communities; always have been, and, I think, always will be.' "

The Island Is Their Playground

One of the most enjoyable ways to explore any island is just to row around it slowly, exploring its many coves and inlets, finding places that you never realized existed from your perspective on shore.

JOYCE MORRELL, who moved to Campobello thirty years ago, when she was ten years old, explains what life on the island is like for its children.

"As soon as I saw the playground [that was built several years ago next to St. Anne's Church] I knew the idea of a playground on this island wouldn't go over because closing these children in a cage, with any kind of fence, is ridiculous. They went there one day and used all the swings, played on everything, and have you ever seen a child in there since? They don't want to be tied down. The island is their playground. It's a marvelous place for children because they're loose and they're free.

"A friend of my mother's who lives up the road, her children have children between nine and thirteen and they live in Winchester, Massachusetts. They cannot walk around the block by themselves. Anywhere they go they have to be supervised: in a car, by a parent, to a specified place, then turned loose in an arena under supervised conditions. They wouldn't even let their little girl walk around the block, and it's a very nice neighborhood. They bring her up here and turn her loose on her bicycle and she goes everywhere and they never think of it. It's sad to think that you can't do that with children.

"When you're young you want to see what's at the end of the trail. If you haven't been on one spot, you want to get there. They have a marvelous childhood here."

During a trip into the woods with her mother to gather evergreen boughs, which will be used to fashion Christmas wreaths, Kimberly Savage offers a friendly smile. ▶

Island kids have always loved to explore their surroundings. They used to do so on foot or horseback. Today many of them use motorbikes. ◆

The library, situated near the seashore at Welshpool, offers children one way to learn about the history of their island home and the world outside its boundaries. ◆

Parents often know just where to find wayward youngsters: at a favorite bend in the road outside Wilson's Beach called "The Rock." ◆

MORRIS &
VARNE FLETCHER

Boatbuilders

BOATBUILDERS Morris and Varne Fletcher often work together in the shop where their father began building boats. But, for the most part, they each build entirely different craft. In his kitchen Varne fashions beautiful models of the tall-masted ships that used to ply the waters of Passamaquoddy Bay, while Morris, who also works at the Jackson Brothers' fish-processing plant, still builds working fishing boats such as the one he is near completing for his son. Made of oak and cedar, the finished boat should cost about ten thousand dollars, not including Morris's labor.

Another island resident, ninety-year-old Asa Brown, recalls that Morris built the first of twenty-five boats that Asa used while he was a fisherman. Says Asa, "I went over and asked him, 'How much would you build me a boat for? I don't want one very big. I want her built twenty-six-foot-long and six-foot-wide.' He said, 'Oh, should be over a hundred dollars.' He built her and painted her. And I went over after and 'Well, now,' I said, 'You said it'd be over a hundred dollars. It don't want to be too damn much over a hundred dollars, cause I ain't got very much over a hundred.' Well, he said, 'I'm going to be as good as my word. A hundred and one dollars.' "

Varne Fletcher

Morris Fletcher ◆

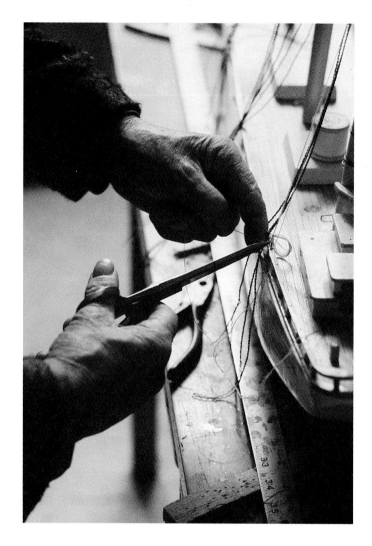

Varne Fletcher works on model ships in his home.

BUD MITCHELL

Fishing and Processing

A LVA "BUD" MITCHELL tells much of his story in verse he composed himself. He is one of six men I met while they were hauling, splitting, boning, salting, and drying fish at the Jackson Brothers' processing plant at Wilson's Beach. The other men are Bernham "Bun" Lank, Waldo Mathews, Morris Fletcher, Neal Langmaid, and Ronald Brown. All but one of them are in their early seventies to mid-eighties. They say most younger men and boys are uninterested in doing their work. "The way it's going around here now, probably by next year, two or three of us will go to sleep and never wake up," and, they believe, Jackson Brothers won't be able to find replacements for them. The older men are proud of their work and feel they do a better job than the youngsters who occasionally work with them and poke fun at them.

When asked if any of them had left Campobello for long, Bud Mitchell replied, "Well . . . I went up to Calais [Maine] one time. Oh, it was good while it lasted. I went in the morning and was home by supper. Didn't want the sun to set on me in a foreign land."

Many Campobello men travel to other places while fishing, sometimes hundreds of miles from their island. Those who still live on the island seem perfectly content to stay there. Perhaps they know something we don't.

Fishing off the coast of Grand Manan, James Tinker uses a gaff, a stick with a metal hook in one end, to help haul in fish from the trawl line being winched aboard his boat. The orange buoys on poles are location markers which hold each end of the long, hook-laden trawl line as it sits in the ocean.

"We used to work over to a place they called the Brine Freeze," Bud says, "They got mostly hake. At that time it was about the only fish they was gettin' in any quantity. So, we went to work over there. Twenty cents an hour. One week I made five dollars and forty cents.

"I used to sing a song about the Brine Freeze but, I don't know, I never tried to recite it. It'd sound kinda foolish, I'm afraid. I wouldn't know the tune now. I could sing it if I had a little accompaniment or something to get it started right.

"It's just like the old feller. He lived over there and he said, 'Oh, I get up in the morning and I start a hummin' and I think, "Well, where did you hear that before?" And I say, "Well, I never heard it before, nor you never heard it before, nor nobody else never heard it before, cause I'm a makin' it up just as I go along. The purtiest music that you ever heard or I ever heard, or anybody else ever heard." '

"Well, 'The Old Hake Song' went,

> Let me tell you a tale,
> A good one I'll make,
> Of a job that I had,
> A filletin' hake.
>
> I was hangin' round town,
> Not earnin' a dime,
> Bein' out of a job,
> Spendin' my time,
>
> When a big guy walks up,
> And he said, 'I suppose
> You're a plain fisherman,
> By the smell of your clothes.'

◀ *Sitting in the stern of his father's small fishing boat, Calvin Malloch hunches up to ward off the chill October wind and rain. Holding a tangled hand line, festooned with a dozen or so hooks, he is waiting for one or more fish to bite before hauling them aboard.*

So I says, 'Yes, you're right,
There's none I ain't caught.
If it's fish that you're talkin',
I'm here on the spot.'

So, he gets all excited,
And I asks what he pays
If I fillet his hake
For a couple of days.

When he offered me twenty,
Said I, 'That is plenty,
Cause the summer's gone by
And I ain't earned a penny.'

So he said, 'All right, Bud,
I'll give you a chance,'
On our feet then we jumped,
And walked to his plant.

For an hour we stayed,
And we talked everything,
And he said, 'Now can any
Of you fellers sing?'

So, I opened my mouth
With the rest of the boys,
And they said, 'Shut it up.
It's a terrible noise.'

I said, 'All right, Rich,
That voice is my own,
And it sounds a lot better
Than your baritone.'

So, we bid him good night
At a quarter t'eleven,
And he told me to show up
Next morning at seven.

I went in the plant
And gazed all around,
And there in the corner
Lay five thousand pound.

Oh, those slimy old hake.
Oh, those slimy old hake.
They're the slimiest fishes
That ever did swam.
You can talk about eels,
And I don't give a damn,
But, oh, those slimy old hake.

So, he put Mire and Dald
On the table to trim.
And Dewey was there,
But I won't mention him.

'Cause you ask all the boys,
And here's what they'll say,
'Dewey ain't got no job,
He's just gettin' his pay.'

Well, Thad Cooke said where he was
There was too much dirt.
He wanted a job
To wear a white shirt.

Baiting trawl lines and mending nets are just two of the many preparations fishermen need to make before going out in their boats.

So, one noon he left,
And he never come back.
He said he got tired
Of wearing a sack.

So, he baited his trawl
And went on the deep haul,
And he went with B. Rice,
A draggin' up coal.

Now every night
He gets down on his knees,
And prays for his job,
Back to the Brine Freeze.

Newt, he wore a big smile
All the time he was hired,
But, oh, the black looks
The day he got fired.

And he told all the boys,
The next time I see Rich,
I'm gonna pound the head off
That son of a bitch.

Pearl Syme; couple of days
After Newt got his time,
We looked down the steps,
And down 'em come Syme.

He's all right makin' boxes.
Or sharpenin' knives,
But you have to look twice
To make sure he's alive.

Oh, we stand there all day,
And we work just like hounds,
And Murray comes down,
And he makes the hake sounds.

When he gets them hung out,
It's true I will swear,
You have to go to the outhouse
For a breath of fresh air.

And Terry said, 'If you boys
Will get out of the way,
I'll soon start up
That old Chevrolet.

'It isn't my fault
If the engine don't go,
'Cause there is nothin' about one,
That I do not know.'

He said, 'She'll go,
You need have no fear,
'Cause I'm the guy
That fixed Hoke's backin' gear.'

We worked all that week
Until Saturday,
And of course all the boys
Were expectin' their pay.

When Bud, he came out,
And he said, very soon,
'The boss will not be here
Until Monday noon.'

Working inside the cabin of his boat, James Tinker and a crew of helpers put small bait-fish on hundreds of hooks strung out on long trawl lines. The lines will be let out consecutively to form one long line, possibly a mile from end to end.

So all of our hopes
Fell flat to the ground,
And poor Puffy said,
'That's a dismal sound.

'Here I worked all the week,
And it's just the beginner,
Now I gotta have fillets
For my Sunday dinner.'

"That's the end of that one. They used to call it, 'The Hake Song,'when I used to sing it. They said, "Aw, sing us "The Hake Song." ' I used to chord it on the piano. People used to laugh at it. I don't know whether they thought it was funny or because I was foolish.

"I used to recite quite a lot 'til one time I was at the factory with one of the fellers I mentioned in that, they called Puffy. He said, 'Used to go lobster fishin' way up north,' and he's talkin' about this fellow. He said, 'Oh, he wasn't a proper damn fool, but he'd recite for you.' So, I thought t'was about time I was quittin' after that.

"I had a chance one time . . . I was gettin' twenty cents an hour and the boss over there told me, 'You write that down for me and I'll give you an hour's pay.' Now, just think, I'd a been in the money today if I'd a went in the publishing business. Twenty cents!

"There was another feller down here one time. He had a boat down here. She smashed up on the beach. I made up a few verses. Used to have fun with Dewey. I used to sing that, too:

Dewey woke up at dawn
And hauled his clothes on,
Just as soon as he jumped from his bed.

When he heard the wind screech,
He made for the beach,
'But I fear it's too late now,' he said.

As he gazed off afar,
He could still see her spar,
And he thought that she was there secure.

But when he got there,
He found in despair,
She was scattered all over the shore.

Well the sea struck the craft,
And it broke her off aft,
And with each one that struck her she'd moan.

He said, 'She's no good
Now except for wood.

With me own nag I'll drag her up home.'

So he shifted her length
Across the beach,
And battered up over the rocks.

It ain't the old craft,
It's the valuable shaft,
And the fans and the good stuffin' box.

Another chore, mending nets, is often done right on the wharves to which the fishing boats are tethered. Alternatively, they might be repaired in the twine shop located at Welshpool.

But when the tide had gone down,
And the beach was aground,
With pieces of old, soggy plank,

He hollered, 'Hey fellers,'
I found her propellers,
Way down in the sand where they sank.'

Then Dewey he hollered,
'We have salvaged her well,'
Expressin' his very best thanks.

And what's drifted up by
Will not miss the eye
Of Peter, Myre, or Banks.

Then Dewey he hollers
He coulda got fifty dollars,
For the boat on the beach where she lay.

But the No'theaster she come
And put her on the bum.
She ain't worth a nickel today."

Processing fish at the Jackson Brothers' plant at Wilson's Beach, Bud Mitchell splits the pollack, hake, and codfish. Then Neal Langmaid showers salt over a layer of fish added to the tank in which they cure. After being removed from the brine tanks, they are laid on racks to air-dry before being cut and packaged.

Sardine Canning

Sardine canning is an assembly-line operation. At the Wilson's Beach plant, the only sardine-canning factory on Campobello, a conveyer belt delivers a seemingly endless stream of herring to scores of women whose flashing scissors snip off the heads and tails before stuffing the tiny fish into cans in which they are cooked.

The canning industry, which began locally over one hundred years ago, once prospered with more than eighteen factories operating in the Lubec-Eastport-Campobello area between the two world wars. At its peak in 1950 the canning industry overall produced more than 3.8 million cases. Production is now less than a third of that.

The women working in the cannery use ordinary household scissors to snip the heads off the sardines before stuffing them into cans in which they are cooked.

One of dozens of labels used to identify sardine brands, this original drawing with watercolor wash was found by Lubec resident Barney Rier, who repairs canning machinery for a living.

During a break in their work day, a group of women relax and enjoy the sun on a stairway outside the Wilson's Beach canning factory.

Lobstermen

Lobstermen on Campobello Island, like Ernest Barker shown painting his buoys, have a limited season, unlike their nearby Maine counterparts. They can only put out their traps from November until May. Many of them sell their catch to the A.M. Look lobster pound at the southern end of the island, where they are stored in a huge tide-washed enclosure for "harvesting" at any time of the year.

Weirmen

Weirmen Edwin "Bud" Allingham and his son Dwight repair one of their weirs located in Friar's Bay off Welshpool. Author Alden Nowlan describes a weir (pronounced ware) as "essentially a pen set up near the shore into which the fish, mostly small herring, swim at high tide and are trapped as the tide recedes. ◗

The construction of a typical weir is evident in this one, located at the mouth of Head Harbor. Through the net's mesh can be seen the Head Harbor Lighthouse, also known as East Quoddy Head Light ➡

"*The first weirs were erected off Campobello in 1840. Fastened to stakes driven into the seabed they were walled in the old days by intertwined brush; today nylon netting is used. The fishermen remove the fish from the weir by dropping a weighted net, called a purse-seine, vertically into the water and bringing its ends together.*

"*Formerly the weirs were given names like ships, and it is said that one of them, called, 'I am alone,' was so christened by one of two partners who felt that he had done more than his share of the work in building it.*"[17]

Shrouded in the cool, blue mist of early morning, this weir is located in the bay adjacent to Friar's Head, named for the outcropping of rock resembling a robed monk deep in contemplation. It was the scene of naval artillery practice during the War of 1812, but the gunners never succeeded in knocking down the head.

Traversing his weir at dawn in a small, powered boat a fisherman tries to determine how many herring are trapped inside the enclosure. Some weirmen use modern, portable, electronic devices to gage the size of their catch. Others still use the old-fashioned method by which they pass through the school of fish holding a weighted, steel wire to determine, by experience, if there are enough fish inside the weir to make it worthwhile to haul them out.

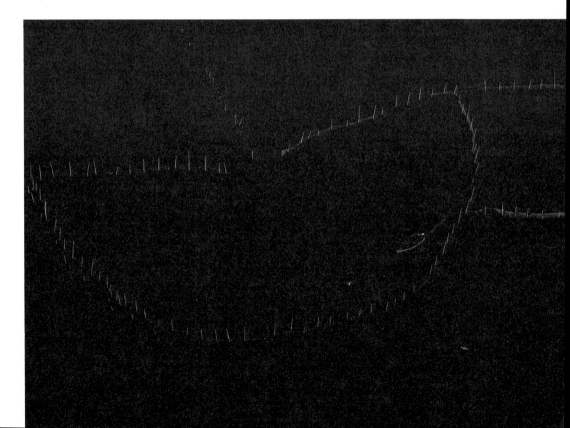

Awash in a sparkling sea of light, a group of Campobello Islanders wait patiently outside a Friar's Bay weir for a glimpse at a small minke whale inadvertently caught in the fish trap. After three days of study by curious residents and a group of researchers from the College of the Atlantic, the whale was released.

113

Reflecting the light of the setting October sun, dead squid litter the beach at Friar's Bay. Since they are useful as bait, fishermen gather the squid, which were lured onto the beach at high tide by the light of street lamps twelve hours earlier.

RAD PIKE:

The Island's Beauties

R AD PIKE, who died suddenly at the age of 75 on August 31, 1979, was one of the most friendly and helpful people I met during my Campobello Island work.

A member of a prominent family from Lubec, Maine, Rad had a doctorate in plant science, a master's degree in horticulture, and served as associate curator of the herbarium at the University of New Hampshire's botany department. An expert on the flora of Campobello and neighboring Washington County, Maine, he acted as naturalist for the Roosevelt Park from 1975 until his death. Before that he was the park's executive secretary for nearly five years.

Rad assisted me by giving me a place to stay in his Lubec home during several of my week-long trips to the area, by offering advice on what plants and natural areas on the island would be most appropriate and photogenic, by suggesting names of people who could help me or who might be interesting subjects to photograph or interview, and generally by being a very good friend.

◀ *Sitting at the head of a magnificent Oriental carpet in his Lubec home, Rad Pike recalls the story of its history and acquisition:*

He purchased the carpet from Ross Skinner, who bought it in 1921 during a visit to Peking. Rad says that, according to a letter given to Mr. Skinner, "The family of the empress apparently looted her warehouses after the dynasty fell." It had been given to the empress's niece "by her foreign secretary as a birthday present and was used in front of her throne for a time as a rug on which to kowtow before the empress."

The design of the carpet is "a tree with storks, clouds, and bats. And there's a pine tree, a plum tree, and a lotus pond at the bottom. They all have a tremendous significance in Chinese mythology. Somebody who knew quite a lot about it said the border looked Tibetan to them. So maybe the thing had been woven in Tibet."

Each evening he was in Lubec, Rad held a cocktail hour in the beautiful, rambling, old house in which he and his sister and three brothers were born and raised. Especially during the summer, but often at other times as well, people from town, other parts of Maine, or other states would attend the informal get-togethers. The conversation was always interesting, animated, and enjoyable, if not downright controversial and, occasionally, outrageous.

Located in Maine's poorest county, Lubec is a small community with severe economic problems. Between World War I and World War II there were as many as eighteen sardine-canning factories in the town. Now there are only two. At the turn of the century there was daily steamship service to Boston and the summer colony on Campobello provided a brisk trade. Now the waterfront and business area is mostly boarded up and much of the town is in decay.

Commenting on the fact that many people leave a dying community for more prosperous areas, Rad once told me, "Some people say, 'The best people left Lubec a long time ago.' Others say, 'No, the best people stayed.' "

Rad Pike certainly was one of the best and, luckily for me and everyone else who knew him, he stayed.

"The island is not unique botanically," Rad explained, "I don't suppose there's a thing that grows on Campobello that is unique to Campobello. You have to set people straight on that immediately.

"The environment of the Bay of Fundy, in which Campobello is situated, is unique because of the fog and the low temperatures. Temperature at night is rarely over fifty degrees, and there's a great deal of fog and humidity in the air. It makes mountain-top

Peering out from the entrance to its silken home, a small spider is engulfed in a veritable galaxy of shimmering water droplets which formed as dew the previous night. ▶

Mushrooms grow on the soft, carpetlike floor of the "Fog Forest" at Liberty Point, where the moisture-laden atmosphere creates conditions similar to those found in tropical rain forests, but at cooler temperatures. ▶

Bright green shoots of grass sprout in organically rich, black soil during spring in the Roosevelt Park's natural area. The small, red plants are sundew, which are carnivorous, the tips of their flowers being coated with a sticky, insect-attracting substance.

119

conditions exist at sea level, which is a very interesting thing. So it means many plants grow well on Campobello that you wouldn't expect to strike until you got much farther north or on mountain tops.

"I doubt there are many parts of the world where you would find that situation. Some of the conditions you find there you wouldn't find until you got to Labrador, probably; certainly, Newfoundland, and these are accessible and those are not.

"We have tremendous areas of sphagnum bog with many, many species of sphagnum and lichens and mosses. We have the type of bog that doesn't necessarily grow out of a pond. Most people thing of bogs as growing from ponds. Our biggest bogs over there did not grow from ponds. Probably started in the woods, because there are remains of forest at the base of the big bog at the Duck Pond.

"The bog is higher in the middle than it is at the edges. You usually don't get this until you get into the northern bogs. The bog is still expanding into the nearby woods in certain directions. There are trees growing in the bogs whose height might not be more than a few feet above the surface, yet their roots go down very low and they might be hundreds of years old. No one's quite sure. They look like bushes; three, four, five feet tall at the most; black spruces ordinarily. The branches take root as the moss comes up so the roots are superficial but, of course, there's very little nourishment in sphagnum. You dig one of them up and take the tree and put it in normal soil and in a few years it'll start growing the normal amount.

"The big bog is fourteen feet deep, and the carbon 14 sample from the bottom of the bog is seven thousand years old, which is a very rapid rate of accumulation. They were figured usually a foot a thousand years. Well, this has been two feet a thousand years.

"You can see the trees being overcome. There's one particular place where it's very obvious the sphagnum is still expanding into the adjoining woods. 'T' isn't all around, because there's a difference in the land elevation.

"The Roosevelt Park bought this land to protect the Roosevelt place. They weren't aware of the unique biological interest that was involved.

"In setting up our drives through the park we tried to follow the old carriage roads that the summer people had. They still wind, and we've tried to keep them at ground level without having them built up. There's one that goes down either side of the island. It's not possible for them to be connected, except way back; but not down at the end, thank heavens, so we won't run into the thing they run into in many European parks where people merely take an automobile circuit of the thing and call it square.

"These two drives we've made are the skeletons from which we will have many walking paths. Among other things, we hope to completely circumnavigate the shoreline.

"There's a great deal of driftwood. This is one of the beauties of a shore like that. It happened just a few winters back that a most unusual storm we had put a lot of driftwood just where we wanted it to block the access to the beach at Lower Duck Pond. That storm removed some land that had been there for a long, long while. There used to be fishermen's camps there. The storm last winter took at least ten feet off it.

While Rad's description of the island, particularly the Roosevelt Park's natural area, is interesting, the only valid way to appreciate Campobello is to walk over it and let it fill your senses to capacity with its beauty.

The sun pierces the heavy fog of Liberty Point at the southern end of Campobello Island. Many of the area's trees are choked with lichen, dripping with condensation. Long-dead trees still stand in many parts of the forest, their stark silhouettes adding to the eerie beauty of the place.

Tipping

◀ *Beth Calder slides her tips onto a long stick to make storage and carrying easier.
Later, Beth, her mother, Marie, and Shelly Jones pile the loaded poles onto
a pickup truck.*

*Tipping is the term used by islanders to describe the process of gathering evergreen
boughs from which Christmas wreaths are fashioned.*

Lenny Lank carefully picks the best tips he can from a rain-drenched tree.

Back at the Calder's home, Lenny's wife, Faye, uses a wire form to start making a Christmas wreath.

Chapter Notes

1. Alden Nowlan, *Campobello: The Outer Island* (Toronto and Vancouver: Clarke, Irwin & Company Ltd., 1975), p. 2. Used by permission.

2. William F. Ganong, Royal Society of Canada, *Proceedings and Transactions*, Second Series, vol. 7 (May 1901), pp. 294–295.

3. Nowlan, *The Outer Island*, p. 10.

4. Ibid., p. 29.

5. Ibid., p. 2.

6. Ibid.

7. Ibid., p. 92.

8. Guy Murchie, *Saint Croix: The Sentinel River* (New York: Duell, Sloane, and Pearce, 1947), p. 246.

9. Nowlan, *The Outer Island*, p. 116.

10. Ibid., p. 80.

11. Harold S. Davis, "International Community on the St. Croix (1604–1930)," *The Maine Bulletin*, 52 (April 1950), p. 301.

12. Nowlan, *The Outer Island*, p. 80.

13. Ibid., p. 58.

14. Ibid., p. 4.

15. Ibid., p. 123.

16. Lois Lowry, "Where FDR Sunned," *The New York Times*, June 1, 1975.

17. Nowlan, *The Outer Island*, p. 67.

Bibliography

Most of the quotations in the introduction are from Alden Nowlan's enjoyable book, *Campobello: The Outer Island*. It is the most complete account I have found of the island, its people, and its history. Much of the information in it is taken from an unpublished manuscript by Mrs. John Gallagher, now a Campobello resident.

Brown, C. Donald. *Eastport: A Maritime History*. Eastport, Maine: International House, Border History Research and Publishing Center, Fathom Series, 1968.

Chapin, William A. R., M.D. *The Story of Campobello*. Self-published, 1960. Available from the Maine State Library, Augusta, Maine.

Davis, Harold A. "An International Community on the St. Croix (1604–1930)." *The Maine Bulletin* 52 (April 1950).

Drake, Samuel Adams. *The Pine Tree Coast*. Boston: Estes and Lauriat, 1891.

Ganong, William F. "Owen's Diary." *Collections of the New Brunswick Historical Society* 1 (1897): 193–220; 2 (1899): 8–27.

Ganong, William F. Royal Society of Canada, *Proceedings and Transactions*, Second Series; vol. 7 (May 1901): 294–295.

Johnson, Ryerson, ed. *200 Years of Lubec History, 1776-1976*. Lubec, Maine: The Lubec Historical Society, 1976.

KILBY, WILLIAM HENRY. *Eastport and Passamaquoddy.* Eastport, Maine: Edward E. Shead and Co., 1888.

LARRABEE, DONALD. "Campobello: FDR's Beloved Island Is a Joy Today." *Maine Sunday Telegram* (June 1, 1975).

LOWRY, LOIS. "Where FDR Sunned." *The New York Times* (June 1, 1975).

MURCHIE, GUY. *Saint Croix: The Sentinel River.* New York: Duell, Sloane, and Pearce, 1947.

MUSKIE, STEPHEN O. "FDR's Beloved Island." *The Biddeford-Saco Journal* (October 30, 1975).

NOWLAN, ALDEN. *Campobello: The Outer Island.* Toronto and Vancouver: Clarke, Irwin and Co., 1975.

PALSITS, V. H., ed. *The Narrative of Captain William Owen, R.N.* New York: The New York Public Library, 1942.

"Roosevelt's Campobello." *The Maine Times* (July 28, 1978).

Tidal Power Study, Cobscook Bay, Maine, USA. Public Information Brochure Prepared for Public Meetings. Waltham, Mass.: Department of the Army, New England Division, Corps of Engineers, 1978.